Sophocles: Women of Trachis

DUCKWORTH COMPANIONS
TO GREEK AND ROMAN TRAGEDY

Series editor: Thomas Harrison

*Also available*

**Euripides: Hippolytus**
Sophie Mills

**Euripides: Medea**
William Allan

**Seneca: Phaedra**
Roland Mayer

**Seneca: Thyestes**
P.J. Davis

**Sophocles: Ajax**
Jon Hesk

DUCKWORTH COMPANIONS
TO GREEK AND ROMAN TRAGEDY

# Sophocles: Women of Trachis

## Brad Levett

## Duckworth

First published in 2004 by
Gerald Duckworth & Co. Ltd.
90-93 Cowcross Street, London EC1M 6BF
Tel: 020 7490 7300
Fax: 020 7490 0080
inquiries@duckworth-publishers.co.uk
www.ducknet.co.uk

A catalogue record for this book is available
from the British Library

ISBN 0 7156 3188 8

Typeset by e-type, Liverpool
Printed and bound in Great Britain by
CPI Bath

# Contents

# Preface

Historically, the *Women of Trachis*[1] has been the odd one out in the extant corpus of Sophocles. It has a plot that allegedly does not possess a unified action, in contrast to Aristotle's (influential) advice.[2] It has two central characters, neither of whom fits well with the general image of the 'Sophoclean hero'.[3] Finally, it has a generally 'archaic' setting of monsters and magic.[4] The play's sympathetic portrayal of Deianeira has often been used as a means to defend the value of the work, but only at the expense of Heracles' portion of the play at the end, since she is absent and largely ignored during this final sequence. Yet past criticisms of the play often resulted from unwarranted assumptions about the nature of Sophoclean tragedy, and of Greek tragedy in general. By questioning a number of assumptions about the play, scholars are arriving at very different views than in the past.[5] When the 'difficulties' of the play are examined without recourse to these assumptions, the strengths of the play can be seen more clearly: a bold plot structure that dramatises the central reversal of the play, a powerful depiction of the force of desire (in the first instance sexual, but desire also for power and reputation) as it operates on both male and female, a critical examination of the institution of marriage, and a grim exploration of the limits of human knowledge.

This book has two objectives. First, it gives the reader the basic background information required to allow her to understand the play. Secondly, by making use of such information in conjunction with the text, it presents a number of interpretations of different aspects of the play in order to suggest how such historical study enlarges our understanding and experience of the work. Rather than give brief accounts of every aspect of the play, I have chosen to examine in more detail those elements of the play I consider to be of particular importance, in order to highlight some of the approaches that can be used when interpreting the work. I have attempted to be pluralistic and to mix old with new: hence traditional approaches such as the study of plot and character are presented alongside more recent approaches such as reception theory and gender studies. At the end of the work will be found a glossary of Greek terms used, and a section on further reading. The notes are intended primarily to direct the reader towards relevant primary and secondary sources. The translations are my own. Finally, I am happy to thank Bill Allan, Ruby Blondell, Martin Cropp, Pauline Ripat and series editor Tom Harrison for reading earlier drafts and making numerous improvements and corrections. I remain responsible for any remaining errors of fact or judgment. This book is dedicated to Yuko.

# 1

# Summary of the Play

An Athenian tragedy is generally structured as follows.[1] First, there is an initial scene before the Chorus enters, called a prologue. The entry of the Chorus, and the song they sing, is referred to as the *parodos*. The scene that follows is called the first episode, the following choral song the first *stasimon* (literally 'standing song', i.e. the first song not sung while entering the performance space, as the *parodos* was); the following scene is termed the second episode, the following song the second *stasimon*, and so on until the end of the play, with the final episode being referred to as the *exodos*. The *Women of Trachis* has four episodes and four choral songs (called *stasima*, in the plural), in addition to the prologue, *parodos* and *exodos*.[2]

The prologue has Deianeira in front of the palace in Trachis,[3] where she and her family are in exile while her husband, the famous hero Heracles, is once more absent on his labours, as he so often has been in the past. She tells of how as a young woman the bestial river god Achelous desired her, and of her fear at such a union (1-25). She explains how her seemingly good fortune at being rescued by Heracles was short-lived, as she lives now in constant fear for her husband as he risks his life on his various labours (26-48). Such is her present situation, having had no word from Heracles for over a year. At this point the Nurse (who has probably been on stage since the start of the play) suggests to Deianeira that she send her son Hyllus to look for his father (49-60). Hyllus enters and tells Deianeira that for a year Heracles has served as a slave to the Lydian queen Omphale, and now, having finished his servitude, is making war against Euboea,[4] the kingdom of Eurytus. Deianeira for her

9

part tells Hyllus that she has a prophecy concerning Heracles, that he is at a critical point in his life and his fate rests in the balance. Learning this, Hyllus leaves to find out the truth about his father's situation (64-93).

In the *parodos*, the Chorus (94-140), a group of young unmarried women of Trachis (hence the title of the play),[5] enters and sings a song relating to a number of themes already raised, such as Heracles' absence and Deianeira's anxiety. They also urge Deianeira to view things more positively, emphasising the changing fortunes of humankind, and suggesting that she should hope for a change for the better. This theme of life's uncertainty was raised by Deianeira in the prologue in relation to her own life, and it will be a dominant one throughout the play (see below, pp. 92-102).

In the first episode Deianeira again tells of her miseries as a wife that result from her fear for Heracles. She contrasts herself to the unmarried Chorus, and also to other married women, asserting that the usual anxiety of a wife for her husband and children is for her many times greater. She also provides a fuller account of the prophecy Heracles gave to her on a written tablet, which stated that if he was not back within fifteen months, his life would end, but if he made it past this crisis he would reach the end of his labours (141-77). At this point a messenger enters and tells Deianeira that Heracles has been successful in his most recent endeavour, and is now returning to Trachis. The Chorus sing a short song of thanksgiving and happiness at the news (205-24), creating a joyous mood that is immediately undermined.[6] For during their song, Lichas (a personal attendant of Heracles) enters leading a large train of women, who are captives from the city of Oichalia in Euboea, which Heracles has destroyed. One of them is Iole, the daughter of Eurytus. Deianeira then asks Lichas for more details about Heracles. Lichas explains that Heracles has not arrived yet because he is currently performing a sacrifice on Cape Cenaeum[7] in thanksgiving for having successfully completed his latest task. Lichas then gives a false account of Heracles' destruction of Oichalia, in order to hide the fact that

Heracles was motivated by lust for Iole (248-90).[8] Deianeira
turns to the captives of Oichalia, expressing sympathy for the
women. She focuses spontaneously on Iole, recognising her as a
'well-born' woman (307-13). Deianeira questions Lichas as to
her identity, but he avoids answering truthfully and Iole herself
does not answer her questions (314-28). Lichas and the captives
enter the palace, and Deianeira is about to follow, when the
messenger tells her that Lichas has lied; he relates to her the
true story of how Heracles sacked Oichalia out of his desire for
Iole, and how this woman is to enter the household as his concubine (335-74). Lichas then returns from the palace, and the
messenger questions him about his story (402-35). Finally,
Deianeira gets Lichas to admit the true tale. She seems
resigned, saying she accepts that desire is a powerful god, and
Heracles is not to be blamed for his actions (436-96). She and
Lichas then enter the palace, with Deianeira promising to send
gifts to Heracles.

The first *stasimon* (497-530) has the Chorus singing of the
power of desire, referring back to the savage battle between
Heracles and Achelous over Deianeira. This song, while it
reminds us of the savage passion that is typical of Heracles, is
also key to understanding Deianeira and her later change of
mind. For the song, with its references to Aphrodite as 'umpire'
(516) of the battle and as the one who 'always carries off the
victory' (497) presents desire as a universal force, which raises
the question of how Deianeira's own desire and jealousy will
affect her (see below, pp. 50-60).

Deianeira returns alone in the second episode bearing a
garment within a casket. She explains to the Chorus that she
has changed her mind, that she cannot endure the idea of
sharing Heracles with Iole, and expresses feelings of jealousy
and inferiority. Deianeira then tells the story of how once, when
she was attempting to cross a river with Heracles, the centaur
Nessus, who was ferrying her across, attempted to sexually
violate her. In response, Heracles shot him with an arrow
covered with the poison of the Hydra. (The Hydra was one of
the mythical monsters Heracles destroyed, whose blood was a

poison Heracles thereafter used on his arrows.) As Nessus lay dying, he told Deianeira to collect his blood because it had the magical property of acting as a love-charm. Deianeira explains that she has kept this blood hidden away in a dark place as the centaur instructed, and has now put it onto a garment which she intends to send to Heracles, in an attempt to win back Heracles' interest (531-87). She hesitates due to the risk and potential shame involved in the use of magic, but, after asking the Chorus for advice, decides to act (588-97). Lichas returns, and she gives the robe to him to take to Heracles. Deianeira enters the palace and Lichas leaves to deliver the robe.

In the second *stasimon* (633-62), the Chorus sing of their desire for Heracles to return home after his long absence, building a sense of happy expectation that is undercut by certain ominous references. The reference to Heracles bringing back spoils (646) reminds us of Iole's presence already in the house, and this combines with the Chorus' return to the theme of Deianeira's suffering in his absence (650-2) to raise audience anxiety over the issue of rivalry between the two women. The final words of the song, while corrupt in the Greek text,[9] seem to have referred to the robe anointed with the Centaur's blood, which no doubt served to remind at least some audience members of the familiar tale of Deianeira killing Heracles by just such a stratagem (for discussion, see pp. 31-2 below).

Deianeira returns in fear in the third episode, explaining how the bit of wool she used to put the blood on the robe, when exposed to the light, shrivelled away and disintegrated. She realises now that it was foolish to trust the centaur. She expresses her resolve to commit suicide if her fears are realised and she has harmed Heracles (672-722). Hyllus returns at this point, having been present with Heracles when Heracles received the robe. Hyllus denounces his mother for destroying his father, assuming that her act was deliberately malicious rather than a mistake (734-7). He reports that Heracles, upon donning the garment as he was sacrificing to his father Zeus, began to be burned alive in it, which ironically turned him from sacrificer to victim.[10] Heracles, now near death, is currently being carried back to Trachis (749-812). To her son's accusations Deianeira makes no response, but silently enters the palace (813-20). Hyllus follows.

The Chorus sing in the third *stasimon* (821-61) of how the prophecy has turned out to be true; for Heracles the two possibilities of dying or of finishing his labours in fact referred to the same thing since it is revealed that death *is* the end of his labours. They refer again to Deianeira's unintentional guilt and her suffering at what has happened. Finally, Aphrodite is 'revealed as the cause of these things' (861), thereby recalling her role as umpire in the first *stasimon*. Just as desire brought Heracles and Deianeira together through violence (Heracles' destruction of the river god Achelous and of Nessus), so too does desire (Heracles' for Iole, Deianeira's for Heracles) ultimately destroy both them and their *oikos* (household).

In the fourth episode, the Nurse enters and tells how Deianeira has killed herself with a sword on her marriage bed, the symbol of her union with Heracles. She also describes how Hyllus, having learned that his mother sent the robe without malicious intent, attempted to stop her, but arrived too late, and so now blames himself for his mother's death (899-946). The Nurse exits. The Chorus then sing in the fourth *stasimon* (947-70) a short song of lamentation for the sufferings of the family, during which Heracles is brought in on a litter carried by attendants, with Hyllus and an Old Man.

The *exodos* begins with the question of whether Heracles is alive or dead (971-92). Heracles awakes, and rages in pain and anger. He demands for Deianeira to be sent to him so that he can kill her. Hyllus explains that she is already dead, and that she acted in innocence in sending the robe, none of which appeases Heracles (993-1142). When Hyllus mentions that Heracles is dying by the machinations of the centaur Nessus, Heracles forgets Deianeira, focusing instead on how the oracles have proved accurate. He says that another oracle stated that he would be killed by the dead, and he now realises that this referred to the cunning of Nessus. He also reiterates that the other prophecy, that he would come to the end of his labours,

13

has also come true, since the dead do not toil (1143-73). Heracles then makes two requests, or commands, of Hyllus. The first is to burn him on a funeral pyre, so as to put him out of his misery. Hyllus promises to see to the deed, although he himself will not perform the act.[11] Heracles then demands that Hyllus marry Iole, to ensure a kind of vicarious possession of the object of his desire. Hyllus is repulsed by the idea, but eventually agrees (1174-1251). The play ends with a sombre procession along one of the *eisodoi* (side entrances) carrying Heracles off to Mount Oeta where he will be burned upon a pyre.[12]

# 2

# Context

## Historical conditions

What we call Greek tragedy is more specifically fifth-century BC Athenian tragedy, and as an art form it is closely tied to the social circumstances in which it originally flourished. Modern western conceptions of art often stress its autonomy. We speak of 'art for art's sake', or the 'intrinsic value' of the piece, or the artist's struggle to realise 'a personal vision'.[1] However, one of the most important general changes in the way scholars study literary texts has been the increasing attention paid to the different historical conditions that produced our texts (including the contexts that produce our own responses to these texts). The use of historicity in the study of literature is not itself new, but in addition to new subjects for historical study (such as social history or the study of cultural meaning), scholars have come to a greater appreciation of just how formative are the specific historical conditions for the production and experience of any art form. Thus the 'historicisation' of literature, meaning simply the study of a work in relation to the conditions in which it was and is experienced, is central to any number of specific theories of literature, including modern interpretive approaches such as reception theory, as well as more overtly 'social' approaches such as gender studies.[2]

A generally historical approach is highly suitable to the study of ancient Greek literature. The ancient Greeks themselves assumed that their various arts were social in nature. Whether we are dealing with the recitation of Homeric epic before a large audience, or the singing of lyric poetry among intimate companions at a private drinking party (symposium), Greek poetry almost always had a social purpose and an intended recipient. Hence it makes sense to try to understand the political, social and ideological[3] conditions that fostered Athenian tragedy in general and that were central in producing the overall effect of the *Women of Trachis* in particular. Thus, in what follows, I outline the chief political, social and ideological factors that gave this text meaning for its original audience, with a view to expanding our own understanding of the play.

### Athenian democracy

The most important political contextual consideration for fifth-century tragedy is the growth of democracy in Athens. The basic political unit of ancient Greece was the *polis*, or city-state, which consisted of an urban centre and the surrounding agricultural countryside. It is important to note that while the various city-states of Greece recognised their shared cultural and linguistic heritage, they were sovereign political entities and often had diverse political and social institutions. Indeed, while the Greeks united in the Persian Wars (490 and 480-79 BC) to repulse Persian invasions of the Greek mainland, they were in fact more often at war with one another in the fifth century. After the Greeks repelled the Persians, the Athenian-led Delian League came into increasing conflict with the Peloponnesian League (made up of Sparta and its allies).[4] The situation between the two sides reached a crisis in 431 BC, when the Peloponnesian League declared war on Athens. This, the Peloponnesian War, lasted, with interruptions, until Athens' defeat in 404 BC. Fifth-century Greece was thus not a unified state in our sense, but rather a culture that linked competing city-states.

Until the end of the sixth century Athens was ruled by wealthy aristocratic families whose power was localised in the land they controlled. However, with the reforms of Cleisthenes at the end of the sixth century there seems to have been a deliberate attempt to structure the state along lines that checked the power of these families. Among other things, Cleisthenes divided the people into ten basic political units ('tribes'), dispersing the localised power of influential families by making these units more representative of Athenian society as a whole.[5] From such beginnings Athens became increasingly democratic as the fifth century progressed.[6] But democracy was both more limited and more extensive than what is usually understood by the term today. Only adult Athenian males could participate in political institutions, and a law passed in 451/0 BC (the Periclean citizenship law), limiting enfranchisement to those male children born of both an Athenian father and an Athenian mother, reveals the sort of anxiety that could exist over just who was allowed to participate. Yet within this limited group, an individual's direct participation in government was much greater than in today's representative democracies, since every adult male could participate in the Assembly and thereby vote on policy.

However, democracy did not simply replace the previous aristocratic form of government but rather overlay and modified traditional aristocratic powers. For within the Athenian democracy it was often still members of the old aristocratic families who had the greatest power in politics. As in many societies, it was the wealthy who had the time to participate in government, and the socially affluent who had the connections and social clout to influence and direct policy. What the democracy did was to make (often aristocratic or wealthy) leaders more accountable in their leadership. For instance, political officials were subject to a scrutiny of their term in office, and an individual could be voted out of power from the more important offices. It is often said that Athenian tragedy projected democratic ideals and concerns against an aristocratic backdrop, since the traditional mythical stories are derived from an aristocratic milieu. Yet in an important way this projection was historically relevant and accurate because contemporary society was itself undergoing the same overlapping of value systems.[7]

### The family

It is very important to take account of ancient Greek perceptions of the family for an understanding of the *Women of Trachis*. The

Greek concept *oikos*, translated as house, household, or family, had both a spatial and a temporal dimension.[8] In its spatial sense, the *oikos* included all the physical property of the family, including slaves and the house itself, as well as the blood relations who lived there. In its temporal aspect, the house also included both the ancestors and descendants of the presently living members.[9] Moreover, just as the possessions and reputation of the family were passed down from generation to generation, so the family had an abiding concern to ensure the continuation of the family at its current (or greater) level of prosperity.

In both aspects the family's primary effect was to impart stability and unity to the community. As a basic building-block of society, it gave position and identity to the individuals who made up the family. One's status and identity in Greek society was in no small part a result of the family from which one was produced, and in turn one's position within the family served to define the individual (as father, son, wife, husband, etc.).[10] On an economic level, the family in its linear historical progression offers a means to divide and distribute a society's possessions in an organised fashion. The production of legitimate heirs as beneficiaries of the family's possessions was therefore one of the most basic functions of the ancient Greek family.

The relation between the family and the *polis* is one of the areas where the aristocratic background of the myths used by Athenian tragedy at first appears to be at odds with the contemporary political realities of Athens. Most Athenian tragedies are about royal families (as is the *Women of Trachis*), and thus the family essentially *is* the state. Consequently the question of legitimate heirs takes on even greater political relevance, since the transfer of the family's wealth includes with it political control of the state. Yet if under democracy political power expressed through (aristocratic) families was reduced, this is not to say that the family no longer functioned as a means for social cohesion. Indeed, once we note the change from power held by a particular family to power held by the people (*dêmos*), the political relevance of the family in fact remains the same. For the lawful institution of marriage, by regulating the produc-

tion of legal citizens, allows for the continuation and mainten-
ance of political power. Thus while the *Women of Trachis* is on
the face of it a strongly domestic drama, we should be aware of
the larger social and political issues at work in it. Questions
dealing with the unity and stability of the family are in fact
political questions for the Greeks, whether viewed from the
perspective of contemporary democratic circumstances of the
audience, or from that of the mythical/heroic past of the plays.[11]

The family itself was controlled by males, and for male interests. A marriage was arranged by the groom and the bride's *kurios*
(the legal guardian of the woman, typically the father), without
reference to the concerns of the young woman herself, who was
typically as young as fourteen or fifteen.[12] While the ideal was that
there would be attraction between the couple,[13] compatibility of
personalities was not the primary concern. Priority was given
instead to the advantages reaped by the families concerned. The
rituals surrounding Athenian marriage reflect this. There was
first a betrothal ceremony between the husband and *kurios*, with
the *kurios* stating the formula 'I give this woman for the
ploughing of legitimate children'. The Greek term for the ceremony of giving away the bride, *ekdosis*, can also mean 'loan', and
this nicely brings out the legal status of the married woman.[14] She
is in a sense 'on loan' to produce legitimate heirs for her
husband's *oikos*. However, she retains her connections to her
natal family, into whose custody she returns in the case of divorce.
Greek texts often refer to the new wife as a 'foreigner' that the
house takes into itself. There is a basic anxiety here resulting from
the fact that the stability and continuance of the *oikos* are dependent upon a woman taken from outside the man's home.[15]

For the wife herself, marriage was one of the key transitions
of her life (as Deianeira herself emphasises in the play, 141-50).
Not only does she pass into a new family, but she also completes
the passage from child to adult. The Greeks tended to think of
children as untamed creatures, and one word for wife (*damar*) is
related to a verb used for taming animals (*damazein*). This gives
a sense of how marriage was understood to train a woman for
her role as an adult wife, at the same time as it conveys a sense

of fear regarding the 'untamed' woman herself, especially her sexuality.[16] Within the family, the role of the wife was to beget and rear children, and to manage the household. One of the defining tasks of women was weaving, or, more broadly, the production of clothing, a time-consuming (and so costly) industry in the ancient world. The importance of fabric production to Athens was emphasised each year in the Panathenaic Festival, when a newly woven, elaborate garment was brought in procession by female celebrants as a gift to place upon the great statue of Athena on the Acropolis.[17] And yet weaving had negative connotations as well. Since weaving was linked by the Greeks with the use of language, and in particular could represent the weaving of deceits and verbal stratagems,[18] it came to represent the perceived deceptive nature of women, a prevalent prejudice within ancient Greek (male) thought. When Deianeira sends Heracles a robe as a gift which ultimately kills him, it is a highly charged symbolic object: as the product of Deianeira's labour, it represents her place in the family and the economic contribution she makes to it, and yet it also potentially represents the perceived capacity of women to deceive, and, as often occurs in tragedy, to envelop and destroy men.

## Reputation and society

The upper-class Athenian male, in contrast to the Athenian woman, led his life largely outside the *oikos*. His role was to conduct business in the marketplace, exercise on the wrestling grounds, do battle on the open field, engage in political deliberation with his fellow citizens, and participate in the religious rites of the city. Thus, while any society will influence the actions of its members by the values and judgments of the group, Athenian society (and ancient Greek society in general) was especially remarkable in the degree to which the individual's value, both to himself and to others, was directly related to how he was perceived by the group. One central Greek cultural value was honour, which meant specifically the degree to which society valued the individual (the primary

Greek term for honour, *timê*, originally meant 'price'). This form of social interaction, where individuals vie with one another for prestige, is often described in terms of a 'zero-sum game', in that an increase to one's honour could only come at the cost of another's.

Indeed, given this high degree of competition, ancient Greece is often described as an agonistic society, and Athenian tragedy itself is a way of enacting, but also of questioning, the relationship between the individual and the group, since it often deals with larger-than-life figures (mythical heroes) who come into conflict with the group. Yet the tension between group and individual is not simply one in which the individual is 'outside society' in the sense of having a different value system from that of the group (tragic heroes are not rebels rejecting society out of rampant individualism). The great individual of tragedy is not always a figure opposed to his/her society, but more often represents some of its most important values, although typically in an excessive form. Ajax, in Sophocles' play of the same name, angered because the armour of Achilles is awarded by the Greeks at Troy to Odysseus rather than himself, attempts to kill them in revenge. Here the Greek contest system and its emphasis on reputation, central to both the heroic world and fifth-century BC Athens, leads to the point that it becomes destructive to society.[19] In cases like this the issue is often one of how to integrate the exceptional figure into the group. Ultimately any society exists in large part to distribute material goods (land, money, possessions) and cultural goods (political power, reputation, status), and Athenian tragedy often examines the individual who would take a greater share but who also potentially has more to contribute. Hence, in Athenian tragedy it is often the heroic individual who is the threat to the group. This is clearly exemplified by Heracles in the *Women of Trachis* since the play questions the role of Heracles in Greek society *after* his civilising labours; for while his labours are seen as a benefit to mankind as a whole, his destruction of the city of Oichalia, motivated by lust for Iole, suggests that his great strength may derive from a wild savagery that has become misapplied and harmful to society. His death in the play may well be taken to suggest that, at this stage, human society is better off without the hero Heracles.[20]

Since they are usually driven by the same value systems as their society, the mythical heroes and heroines of tragedy have an abiding concern for their fame or reputation. Today reputation is often understood as a superficial factor that can, if anything, distort our understanding of the 'true' self. However, the ancient Greeks generally were more accepting of the notion that the individual *is* in large part a social figure. That is, how others saw and judged any given person was not somehow neatly separate from an inherent personality or character; rather the persona created by public opinion *was* in large part the individual. Further, reputation can survive a person after death, and thus can be understood as a type of immortality. The fifth-century historian Herodotus in the opening line of his *Histories* (not far in time from the original performance of the *Women of Trachis*) says that he is writing in part so that 'the things done by men may not be lost to time, and that the great, awe-inspiring deeds of both the Greeks and the barbarians may not become unknown'.

This issue of the individual and the perception of him or her in the eyes of the group is one that is played out in Athenian tragedy in a highly self-reflective fashion that can be understood as a means to bridge the distance between a mythic/aristocratic past (play) and a more democratic present (audience). This occurs because the heroes on stage, in their concern for the opinion of others, and in particular of posterity, are ultimately addressing the contemporary audience in a very direct way. Thus in a sense Athenian tragedy's use of a mythic past allows this past to address its own posterity, since the contemporary audience are in effect the judges of the reputation for which the tragic figures struggle. And since the audience themselves share this concern with social recognition, they can see their own concerns enacted in the drama itself – their concern with self-perception by their contemporaries, and their concern for their own posthumous reputations. Hence the fundamental issues of public display, and the public's censure or approval, are important aspects linking past and present within the genre.[21]

Finally, there is a basic Greek ethical stance which is often described as 'helping friends and harming enemies'. Interpersonal relations between individuals could be defined by two basic categories, that of the *philos* (friend/family member/associate) and that of the *ekhthros* (personal enemy). *Philoi* were those who owed favours and benefits to one another, and were not always those who had a close emotional tie to the person (as we understand the term 'friend'). Its logical (if destructive) converse was the active attempt to do harm to one's *ekhthros* (a person who has harmed you gratuitously in some way).[22] As Aristotle emphasised, Athenian tragedy often turns precisely upon the violation of the bond between *philoi*.[23] Thus, when Deianeira, in response to Iole's introduction into her home, says 'such things has Heracles ... given me in return from my long service' (540-2), she is specifically suggesting that Heracles, as a *philos* who owes her for the benefits she has given him (most of all, children), is failing in his responsibility to her; in sum, that she is getting a bad deal in this personal transaction.[24]

## Athenian drama

As a civic institution within a progressively more democratic state, Athenian tragedy exhibited a level of social interaction and integration that goes beyond any form of drama familiar to us today. First, the plays were performed at religious festivals, particularly at the Greater or City Dionysia held in honour of the god Dionysus. This six-day festival would include religious rites such as animal sacrifices and processions, as well as dramatic and musical performances in different genres. These dramatic performances were themselves a type of offering to Dionysus (in his role as patron god of performance), although they were not themselves rituals.[25] The Athenians took the opportunity to display prominently that year's tribute from the other members of the Delian League, thereby giving the festival a clear political aspect as well. Other ceremonies included the awarding of suits of armour to the sons of fathers who had died in battle, or crowns to reward public benefactors.[26] Further, the festival was held in the spring when the shipping season started, and thus at a time when a number of foreigners would be present, and this timing can be understood as one part of an overall attempt by the state to impress others (and itself) with the economic and artistic wealth of the city, as well as its military and political power. Finally, in keeping with the agonistic nature of Greek life, the poets and their plays were judged and the winners awarded prizes.[27]

Just as Athenian tragedy in its performance setting reflected a range of social concerns (artistic, militaristic, political, financial, religious), this inclusivity was also mirrored in the make-up of its audience. Educated estimates place the attendance at a performance as high as 15,000-20,000 spectators, out of a citizen population of perhaps 30,000-50,000, and a total population of about 300,000.[28] The majority of this audience would have been made up of male Athenian citizens, but it also included slaves, children and, as noted, foreigners. What is still unclear is the crucial question of whether women were in attendance as well.[29] It is important to recognise that if women were present, as many now think, they were not likely to have been present in great numbers. The plays themselves are generally directed towards the male citizens of the audience. The size of the audience, and its relatively inclusive aspect, would have been emphasised by the fact that the plays were performed out of doors during the day, and indeed it seems clear from a number of anecdotes that a dramatic performance was very much a place to see and be seen.[30] The front rows of the audience included important figures, such as the men holding government offices that year, priests, and the judges chosen to award the prize for the competition among the plays.[31]

It is important not to over-generalise the nature of this (or any other) audience, while still recognising that the Athenian audience was likely to have possessed a high degree of conformity among its members in their understanding, appreciation and experience of the work. In addition to the generally public nature of Athenian society, with its emphasis on the intersection of public opinion and personal reputation, since the performance itself was large-scale and out of doors, there was no doubt a certain degree of 'mob mentality', whereby dominant responses within the crowd were adopted by the hesitant.[32] This effect would have been strengthened by the fact that Athenian audiences tended to be unrestrained in their response to the drama they were watching. However, it needs to be emphasised that no language, and no art form, is ever transparent in its meaning or effect. Language and art do not function as seamless systems of communication, whereby what the poet puts in at one end comes out identically for the receiver at the other. Moreover, as we noted, the Athenian audience was clearly made up of different segments of Athenian society (different by wealth, status, nationality and perhaps gender). It is therefore likely that there was a plurality of responses from different members of the audience. Moreover, while the attempt to understand a work within its historical context is an important one, we should not assume that this means that a historical reconstruction of a work will produce a singular answer. It is tempting to assume that if we knew the response/view of *the* audience, we would know *the* meaning of the work (since the work was designed for consumption by this specific audience), but historical reconstruction does not produce a singular answer because the audience of a work of art is never simply a singular entity, even when we can argue that a given audience has a higher degree of social conformity than we might expect from our own experiences.[33]

The Chorus adds a further dimension to the inclusiveness of Athenian tragedy. The members of the Chorus were made up not of 'professional' performers, but of citizens trained for a particular performance. The task and expense of training the Chorus was assigned by the state to wealthy citizens (termed *khorêgoi*) who thereby gained honour and reputation, while the state gained a source of resources for the hugely expensive festivals.[34] Similar to the democracy itself, the Chorus represents society in a limited fashion: it clearly reflects the audience, since its members are drawn from this audience, but of course it is only drawn from the dominant subgroup of society, Athenian male citizens. Often, but not invariably, the Chorus is sympathetic to the main character or characters. More interestingly, it is often made up of what can be described as marginalised segments of society, such as old men, women or slaves. This marginality is perhaps one way that Athenian drama included those segments of society that were not so directly reflected in the actions and concerns of the characters themselves. Whereas the mythical/aristocratic characters of the drama reflect the dominant segment of Athenian society (male citizens), the Chorus represent that larger, but more marginalised and so largely silent, portion of the population. The Chorus should therefore not be seen simply as a stand-in for the historical audience and its responses, nor as some sort of ideal audience (i.e. the response of the Chorus to the action should not be understood simply as the 'correct' response), although it is clear that the Chorus does serve as a structural element, bridging the distance between spectator and performance.[35]

The choral music and dancing are those aspects of Athenian tragedy which are most lost to us today, dependent as we are on the written text. The words of the songs in our texts made up only a part of the original dramatic effect produced by the Chorus, as a group of twelve or fifteen members would have sung these songs to the accompaniment of music, while dancing in elaborate costumes. The music was probably primarily in the form of direct accompaniment, following closely the metrical structure of the words themselves. The dancing was probably of a mimetic nature, whereby choral movements would reflect, in some figurative fashion, the social role of the choral character and the thematic content of the song.[36] A good part of the enjoyment of an Athenian tragedy would have derived from the spectacle provided by the Chorus.[37] Indeed, not only were choral performances of all types common in ancient Greece, since they were one of their primary forms of religious and artistic performance, but the genre of tragedy itself is often understood to have developed out of choral performance.[38]

## 2. Context

The Chorus and the characters were all played by Athenian male citizens. All actors wore a full mask, modelled along naturalistic lines, which covered the whole of the head. Costumes were elaborate and were probably indicative of status. All speaking parts in the play were divided between three actors, and as a result there can only be three speaking parts on stage at any given time (a condition often called the three-actor rule). The most interesting aspect of this division of parts for the *Women of Trachis* is that the roles of Deianeira and Heracles would have been performed by the same leading actor. The actor playing Hyllus probably would also have handled the role of Lichas, with the third actor probably playing the Nurse, the Messenger and the Old Man. (Note also that the three-actor rule means that in the first episode Iole cannot speak.) Style of acting is another area about which we know much less than we would like. However, given the size of the audience and the need to communicate clearly at a considerable distance, gestures and movements presumably must have been fairly obvious and direct.[39]

The theatre was made up of a large semicircular section for seating, set upon a slope to allow visibility. The seating faced the *orkhêstra*, the large flat area (either circular or rectangular in the fifth century) where the Chorus performed. Across the *orkhêstra* from the audience was the performance space for the actors. The *skênê*, a wooden stage building, was located at the back of the performance area. It is not clear whether or not there was a raised stage in the fifth century. The *skênê* itself was a building into and out of which actors could make entrances and exits, and in which costume changes could be made. It could represent any sort of locale, such as a cave in Sophocles' *Philoctetes*, although most often, as in the *Women of Trachis*, it represents a royal palace. On either side of the *skênê* was a path, called an *eisodos* (plural *eisodoi*), which was used for other entrances and exits. Probably each of these two paths represented a consistent location. In the *Women of Trachis*, one path is understood to lead towards the sea and the Malian coast, from where Heracles, Lichas and the captive women of Oichalia arrive. Hence this is the path used predominantly in the course of the play. The other path is understood to lead inland towards Mount Oeta where Heracles will be burned upon the pyre, and hence is used for the final exit of the play.[40]

To conclude our general account we can describe an Athenian tragedy as socially inclusive and yet still clearly socially stratified, orientated towards spectacle in a way that is often lost for us in our dependence upon the written text, socially involved often in both content and its context, and culturally esteemed without being (simply) elitist. A recent account aptly describes the art form as combining 'the ethical status of a public institution (both civic and religious), the broad popularity of a Hollywood blockbuster, the emotional and competitive appeal of a major sporting event, and the artistic and cultural eminence of Shakespeare'.[41]

## Sophocles

Sophocles (*c*. 495-406/5 BC) was historically the second of the 'big three' dramatists of fifth-century Athenian tragedy, although his career in fact overlapped with both his predecessor Aeschylus (*c*. 525-456) and his younger contemporary Euripides (*c*. 480-406). What we know of his life shows that he was very much involved in the social, political and religious affairs of the city. His life encompassed much of the turbulent fifth century: as a teenager he would have heard firsthand of Greece's surprising victory over the Persians in 480/79 (in fact he is said to have danced in a civic celebration of the victory); he was a contemporary of Pericles, the most important politician of Athens in the fifth century; and he died just a year or so before Athens' defeat at the hands of the Spartans in the Peloponnesian War (404 BC). Of his civic career, we know that he was a public treasurer in 443/2, was elected a general for the Samian war (which began in 441), and was elected one of the ten commissioners assigned to reorganise Athenian affairs after their costly defeat in Sicily in 413.[42]

His career also encompassed a time of development in the genre of Athenian tragedy. Aristotle tells us that Sophocles himself introduced the speaking third actor (hitherto only two speaking characters were allowed on stage at any one time) and the practice of scene-painting.[43] He may also have increased the number of the Chorus from twelve to fifteen.[44] Sophocles was both highly prolific and highly successful. The seven complete tragedies we have are only a small fraction of his total output, which consisted of about 120 works.[45]

Since antiquity the traditional account of Sophocles as a dramatist presents him as occupying, artistically, the middle ground between Aeschylus and Euripides. Aeschylus was seen as the grand old man of the theatre, full of high-flown drama and lofty diction, painting, as it were, his plays with a broad, forceful brush. Euripides is, in this systematised and simple picture, the innovator and 'modernist', understood as working in a more self-conscious and even precocious manner, questioning traditional social values and introducing the 'new learning' of the Sophists.[46] While it is true that the works of Euripides do reflect a spirit of intellectual questioning similar to the Sophists, such an influence can be seen in the works of Sophocles as well. As one example, the Sophists' keen interest in the question of whether things occurred due to nature or to culture/society can be seen to have influenced Sophocles' late play *Philoctetes*, where the young man, Neoptolemus, must choose between the deceptive practices which Odysseus teaches him (culture) and his own sense of honesty derived from his being the son of Achilles (nature). Owing no doubt in part to his intermediate position within this continuum of artistic styles, Sophocles is often understood as the most 'balanced', 'ideal' and 'serene' of the dramatists. While this schema owes something to the presentation of the three dramatists in the comic poet Aristophanes' famous play *Frogs*, performed in 405 BC, it is likely to have had some basis at least in popular conceptions of the day. Also, Sophocles has often been depicted as being highly pious, and it has been assumed that this piety is reflected in his tragedies. Albin Lesky wrote of 'Sophokles' profound piety, which has impressed his audiences since antiquity', and of how 'the poet ascends to the level of a piety that plumbs the greatest depths of all the misery in men's helplessness, yet despite these terrors and in their very midst, his piety still finds reverence for the gods'.[47] The *Women of Trachis*, while it is sometimes vaguely understood as an 'old-fashioned' or early play, serves as an excellent counter-argument to such traditional views; for it is neither balanced, nor serene, nor particularly pious, and thus we can leave aside this general view in order to pursue a specific understanding of this play.

### The myth: earlier treatments of Deianeira[48]

This play tells the story of the death of the hero Heracles at the hands of his wife Deianeira, who unwittingly sends him a poisoned robe. But the story of the death of Heracles was only one out of a series of tales linked to this hugely popular figure, including tales of his birth from Zeus, king of the gods, and Alcmene, a mortal woman; tales of the animosity of Zeus' jealous wife Hera, and thus his subsequent labours; and tales of his later elevation to divinity after his death. Moreover, it must be emphasised that any one story had many different versions within a variety of media.[49] Before the *Women of Trachis* there was no single definitive account of the death of Heracles for the poet to adhere to or adapt, but rather a whole range of different stories, most sharing some important elements, but with considerable room for adaptation and innovation.

By examining some of these preceding versions of the tale and the ways that they resemble and differ from the version given in Sophocles' play, we can get both a better idea of the focus that the poet has given to his treatment, and a sense of some of the expectations that might have informed the original audience's response.[50] As Peter Burian has recently phrased it, 'a tragic plot inheres not simply in a poetic text, but also in the dialectic between that text in performance and the response of an informed audience to the performance as repetition and innovation'.[51] In particular for the *Women of Trachis* it is useful to consider the likely extent of the audience's knowledge of the myth in the matter of the characterisation of Deianeira.

30

## 2. Context

While the myths were fairly consistent in presenting Deianeira as the cause of Heracles' death through the object of the robe, the specifics of the story were fluid, particularly surrounding Deianeira's motivation and purpose in sending the robe. The epic versions of Deianeira's character (our earliest evidence) seem to have presented her as an aggressive, warlike figure (perhaps even an Amazon), making her a suitable consort for the aggressive and warlike Heracles.[52] Indeed, her very name in Greek means 'man-killer' or even 'husband-killer'. Earlier portrayals on vases tend to show her in a more active role in the episode of the attack of Nessus, holding the reins of a chariot or escaping from the centaur on her own (in Sophocles she is completely passive and only saved by the arrows of Heracles).[53] Such an aggressive figure suggests that the earlier epic Deianeira killed Heracles willingly, in revenge for his taking Iole and bringing her into Deianeira's home. Such a story type is relatively familiar in Greek myth, as in the case of Clytemnestra who kills her husband Agamemnon. Such characterisation may be conveyed by an important fragment of the *Catalogue of Women* (a sixth-century work that comes down to us under the name of Hesiod):

> ... and she acted terribly, greatly [deluded] in mind,
> and [anointing] the poison on the robe
> she gave it to Lichas, the herald, to [convey. He brought]
> it to his master, [Heracles, sacker of cities,] son of Amphitryon.
> On receiving it, [death's end quickly] came to him,
> [and] he died and went to the [sorrowful] house of Hades.
>
> MW Fr. 25, lines 20-5

The text inside the brackets consists of words supplied by scholars that are missing in the original text. While most of these supplements are trustworthy in sense, the most important word, 'deluded', showing Deianeira's motivation, is less secure, and even if the supplement here is accepted, the word in Greek can refer either to a mistaken intention or deliberate malice. However, the rest of the passage does not suggest any sense of a mistake, and there is no indication that Deianeira was deceived in her use of the drug. What we appear to have is a straightforward act of murder.

With these considerations in mind, it has often been thought that the *Women of Trachis*' presentation of Deianeira as a victim of deception by the centaur (and thus unintentional in her destruction of Heracles) was a mythic variation specifically invented by Sophocles. However, there is also a poem by Bacchylides to consider, since it gives a version of the story similar to that of the play, with Deianeira being deceived by the centaur. Bacchylides 16, lines 23-35, says that while Heracles was sacrificing on Cenaeum,

> Then the irresistible *daimôn*
> wove a clever and
> grievous plan for Deianeira,
> when she learned the sad news
> that the son of Zeus, who fears no fight,
> was sending to his splendid home
> white-armed Iole as his wife.
> Ah, ill-fortuned wretch, to have devised such a thing!
> Powerful envy and the murky veil
> of the future destroyed her,
> when she received from Nessus
> the god-sent monstrosity on the rosy Lycormas.[54]

Here problems of dating come up; since we have no firm date for either work, and since the two poets' careers overlap, either could have influenced the other, or both could be drawing on an independent tradition. Edwin Carawan has recently raised again the question of the relation between the two works, arguing that Bacchylides 16 represents a tradition independent from Sophocles, and thus that Bacchylides' poem is not derived from Sophocles' play. This argument is in part based on the view that Bacchylides' poem represents an 'unequivocally guiltless' Deianeira.[55] Yet while the poem certainly presents a Deianeira different from her vengeful, aggressive epic incarnation (such as in the *Catalogue of Women*), the poem does not present a completely blameless Deianeira. While the reference to an 'irresistible *daimôn*' that wove the device for Deianeira may at first suggest something purely external to Deianeira which forced her action, the term here does not seem to refer to any specific god, but rather to Deianeira's 'fate', a common meaning of the word. And it is clear from the reference to 'powerful envy' (i.e. Deianeira's) that Deianeira's fate is produced, at least in part, *through* her own agency and is not simply independent of it, since the reference to envy suggests that Deianeira's own emotional state led to her action.[56] This sense of Deianeira's agency (and so culpability) in the poem is emphasised if we consider that the *daimôn* is said to have 'woven' a plan, inducing one to think of Deianeira herself, since it is she who (presumably) wove the robe. Also, the line 'Ah, ill-fortuned wretch, to have devised such a thing!' seems clear enough in attributing the plan to Deianeira herself, even if she was under the influence of an overmastering emotional state (which the Greeks often viewed as both a part of the agent, and simultaneously as an external force or god). Finally, the Greek word for 'plan' in the phrase 'wove a ... plan (*mêtin*) for Deianeira' (in reference to the *daimôn*) is etymologically derived from the same root as the word for 'devised' in the phrase 'to have devised (*emêsat[o]*) such a thing!' (in reference to Deianeira), hence again suggesting that the two are to be equated. On the other hand, there is clearly also some sort of mistake made on Deianeira's part, as implied by the reference to 'the murky veil of the future'. Thus, as often in Greek thought, Deianeira's action can be understood to be motivated both by human and by divine will, by both internal and external forces.

Thus the mixture of guilt and innocence we will see in the *Women of Trachis* can also be found here in the Deianeira of Bacchylides' poem. 'Powerful envy and the murky veil/ of the future' suggests that Deianeira killed Heracles unintentionally, due to her inability to see/predict the future, and yet that she did act out of jealousy. Moreover, the Greek term used here for 'envy' (*phthonos*) suggests not so much a desire to win Heracles back as a desire to harm him due to injured feelings, since the term also means 'malice' or 'ill-will'. I suggest that this indicates a narrative plot in the Bacchylides poem different from both previous epic versions and also from Sophocles' version in the *Women of Trachis*: Bacchylides 16 may represent a version of the story whereby Deianeira originally sent the garment she received from the centaur to *Iole*, in a deliberate attempt to kill her rival. The basic story-type is familiar enough in itself, and recalls stories like the *Medea* of Euripides, in which Medea specifically sends to Jason's new wife a wedding garment that is purposely designed to kill her (and does).[57] However, if my speculative reconstruction is correct, here the mistake occurs: Iole, for whatever reason, passes on the robe to Heracles,[58] and the attempted murder of the rival results in the death of the husband. This interpretation is supported by a vase, dated to *c.* 440-430, and discussed by Carawan,[59] which shows a younger woman giving a robe to Heracles as he takes off his traditional garb, a lion skin. On the other side of the vase stands an older woman. As Carawan notes, against Beazley's interpretation, the younger woman is likely to be Iole, and the older woman Deianeira. The importance of Iole handing over the robe to Heracles could represent a mistake in recipient. Otherwise, having Iole hand over the robe adds no important narrative detail. Hence I would agree with Carawan that Bacchylides' poem represents a different mythic tradition both from the epic version (whereby Deianeira kills Heracles in vengeance) and from Sophocles' version (whereby she mistakenly kills Heracles while attempting to win him back with what she believes is erotic magic), but not that it presents a completely innocent Deianeira. Rather, here we have a jealous, vengeful Deianeira who attempts to win back Heracles by the simple expedient of killing her rival.[60] Such a mythic version can be seen as occupying something of a transitional position between the epic and Sophoclean versions of the character.

If this argument has any merit to it (and it remains conjecture), it is highly suggestive of the plurality of narrative options that a given 'standard' myth could offer to the poet, since all these different variations should be understood as available to the poet to call to mind within at least some of his audience. Hence when we come to examine the character of Deianeira and her indecision, and final decision, in the face of the threat of another woman in her house, it will be seen that the drama arouses audience expectation over just this range of possible characterisations. Hence with the *Women of Trachis* we have good evidence against the reductive view that 'the audience already knew the story', and thereby experienced a lowered level of interest towards the events of the play. Rather, in regard to the character of Deianeira, it can be seen how previous versions of the story need not be understood as impediments to dramatic and narrative excitement, but can in fact *increase* audience interest, specifically by offering different narrative avenues that the audience can imagine the tragedy taking, while yet keeping them in suspense over just how the events will turn out.

### Date of original production

We have no firm evidence for the date of the play, with one commentator giving a range from 457 to 430 BC.[61] It has often been dated towards the early part of this temporal range, partially because the play is perceived as generally more 'primitive' in nature. Three basic arguments are at hand: first, simply that the play, with its monsters, magic and brute physicality, has something of the nature of a folk-tale. Yet as has been noted,[62] this so-called 'archaic' aspect may be more a result of the subject matter (in particular Heracles, who is liable to such a treatment due to his role as the individual who overcame archaic, primitive monsters), than a result of the place it occupies within Sophocles' career. A second argument is that there is less dialogue (and in particular less three-way dialogue), and as a consequence longer narrative and choral passages. Since it is often argued that tragedy developed out of choral performance, and since there was a general trend in the fifth century for dialogue to take an increasing share of the play, this would suggest an earlier date.[63] However, the play is very self-reflective about itself as a myth, and subsequently an important theme of the work is storytelling and narrative, and thus this could also explain why the *Women of Trachis* is as it is.[64] Thirdly, the clear two-part structure of the work has suggested to some an earlier date, by the argument that this diptych ('twofold') structure represents a less self-assured handling of the plot.[65] However, it will be seen that the plot structure of the work can be understood as a highly effective one, even if not a 'classically' unified one.

The play is also sometimes given an earlier date due to a connection with Aeschylus' trilogy the *Oresteia*, performed in 458 BC. This connection can be seen both in some particulars (some phrases in the original Greek of the *Women of Trachis* seem to be borrowed from the *Oresteia*)[66] and in the structure of one important scene, Deianeira's confrontation with the silent Iole, which seems to be patterned on Clytemnestra's meeting with the silent Cassandra in the first play of the *Oresteia*, the *Agamemnon*. Yet none of these observations guarantees an early date. There is no reason why Sophocles in the *Women of Trachis* could not have used material from the *Agamemnon* long after the older play's original production, for artistic reasons other than that of drawing the audience's attention to the earlier work. Thus what we sometimes assume are allusions in the *Women of Trachis* to the earlier play may simply be artistic borrowings.

Hence while many would continue to argue for an early date for the *Women of Trachis*, it should be emphasised that the evidence does not admit of a final answer. More importantly, we should not fall prey to the assumption that the mere possibility that the play is an early one in the career of the poet implies a less assured handling by its author. This type of assessment, which amounts to a sort of generalised biographical interpretation, is best avoided in favour of an assessment of the play itself, with its own shortcomings and successes, whatever these may be.

# 3

# Plot[1]

The basic story-line of the *Women of Trachis* is one familiar to
Greek literature and to Athenian tragedy, the *nostos*, or 'return'
plot.[2] The most famous example is the *Odyssey*, which tells the
story of Odysseus' return to his home in Ithaca twenty years
after leaving for the Trojan war. Similarly, there was a collection of epics, the *Nostoi* ('Returns'), dealing with the other
heroes at Troy and their attempts to return home. Within
Athenian tragedy examples of plays exhibiting the *nostos* plot
are Aeschylus' *Agamemnon*, which dramatises the Greek leader
Agamemnon's return from Troy, and Sophocles' *Electra*,
dealing with Orestes' return to his homeland from exile.

In the *Women of Trachis*, the central action is Heracles'
return to Trachis, a return which should be joyous but instead
causes the hero's downfall.[3] The plot creates tension concerning
the anticipated reunion of husband and wife in two main ways.
First, while it is reported as early as lines 185-6 that Heracles
is safe and shortly to be expected in Trachis, this return is
delayed until line 967. Secondly, and directly connected with
this creation of dramatic suspense, are the various ways in
which the return of Heracles, happily anticipated by Deianeira,
the Chorus and (presumably) the audience, becomes compli-
cated and compromised. The plot involves a slow revelation of
information whose validity is uncertain at first, thereby
delaying both the characters' and the audience's understanding
of the true state of affairs.

The notion of human uncertainty in the face of a changing
world is a central theme of the play. It is introduced immediately, when Deianeira relates the typical Greek belief that one

should not assess someone's life until it is over and all of life's vicissitudes have been endured (1-5):

> There is an old account known among humankind
> that you cannot know a mortal's life, whether
> it is good or it is evil, until a person dies.
> And yet I know I have an unhappy and oppressive one
> even before going down to the halls of the dead.

The play will ultimately reveal Deianeira's view to be inadequate, since the tragic resolution of the play will be even worse that what her pessimistic nature leads her to expect, showing that fortune can surprise even those who would attempt, by acknowledging this mutability, to insulate themselves from such reversals.[4]

This opening sets the tone for the plot's emphasis on changing fortune.[5] This notion is repeatedly emphasised in the course of the play, both by the reversals of the plot itself, and by direct comment, such as in the *parodos* (126-36):

> For the king who rules all,
> the son of Kronos,
> did not set a pain-free life for mortals,
> but both pain and grace
> circle around upon all,
> like the whirling paths of the Great Bear.
>
> For neither shimmering night, nor ruin,
> nor prosperity hold constant for mortals,
> but at once they are gone,
> and gladness and deprivation
> come in turn to another.

However, the reversals of the play are often not so much a result of changing conditions or new events. Rather it is often the limits in human knowledge which creates different responses to existing conditions. Thus the Chorus break into song at line 205 at the news of Heracles' safe return, only for this happy mood to be undermined shortly afterwards by the further revelation that he is bringing with him another woman. Hence this dramatic reversal is not effected by a new event, but by a new piece of information which makes both the characters and the audience see the original event (here Heracles' return) in a different light. (For a fuller exploration of this kind of dramatic sequence, see Chapter 5.) Thus the pacing of the plot, with its dramatic revelations of important information, enacts the play's fundamental theme of humankind's inability to see things clearly for what they are.

The plot of the play is also notable for the abrupt break it contains at 946, when the Nurse has reported Deianeira's suicide, and Heracles has not yet arrived, since this means that the two characters never meet on stage.[6] As David Seale notes, Deianeira's 'final departure, which comes at a pivotal point in the play, visibly ruptures the expectations of the development, and so the prospective meeting to which everything has been directed is aborted'.[7] This break between the first part of the play focusing on Deianeira and the second on Heracles is the most striking and commented-upon aspect of the plot, and has often served as a source of criticism of the play. While there have been attempts to link the two parts in various ways, there seems no reason to try to explain away this jarring plot movement, unless we choose to assume that a seamless unity of plot is the highest goal of a dramatic work.

This question of unity in an artistic work is worth pausing over for a moment. The assumption of unity as a measure of a successful or good work has been one of the great blind spots of interpretation. The ideal of unity serves as a comfortable aesthetic standard, for like all such first principles, it often goes unquestioned and even unexplained. Commonly artistic unity is thought to be productive of 'good art'. Yet this is simply an assumption, as there is no objective standard by which it could be shown that unity is somehow necessarily better than disunity, unless unity is understood simply to *be* the goal of any piece of artwork, in which case the argument is either arbitrary or circular. Perhaps a better initial starting point would be simply to say that unity and disunity can be employed to different effects and purposes. For instance, the film *Apocalypse*

*Now*, directed by Francis Ford Coppola, is highly episodic in its plot structure, but this sort of dramatic pacing helps to convey a sense of madness and chaos in war. In addition to this general question of the overvaluing of unity as an aesthetic criterion, there is also the question of what *type* of unity is to be applied. On a historical level, even for those Greek intellectuals who did favour unity in artworks (e.g. Aristotle and Plato), this unity seems to have been more of a formal unity than a thematic unity.[8] In the case of the *Women of Trachis*, it is perhaps the lack of a unity of character more than anything else that offends modern sensibilities, since the break in the plot structure entails a strong shift from one character to another. Finally, we should beware of taking a work that, for whatever reasons (the reputation of the artist, the praise of past generations, personal experience, etc.), is already considered to be of high quality, and then assuming that the work should therefore be unified in some fashion so as to justify this initial valuation of the work. For the interpreter may simply construct the unity he or she assumes should be there.

Thus, rather than trying to find a way to knit together the two parts of the play, and rather than condemning the play should we not be able to do so (e.g. 'the play is an immature work', 'the play ends with an awkward coda on Heracles'), it is more valuable to ask what effect this rupture of the plot can be seen to have in its own right. Pat Easterling and others have approached the play in this fashion.[9] The rupture can be seen as a powerful dramatisation of the breakdown in the union of Heracles and Deianeira, since the extent to which the unifying bond of marriage in this play comes to serve a destructive function can virtually be measured by the performance area itself; the home where the envisioned happy reunion of the family was to occur ultimately comes to portray the empty space where they will in fact never be gathered (compare 1151-4). Hence this aspect of the plot helps to add impact to the play's tragic reversal. For, given the expectation created by the audience's pre-existing knowledge of the story, the movement from a happy to a tragic homecoming cannot be understood as wildly surprising. However, by use of this bold rupture in the plot, Sophocles is able to reinstall, as it were, a sense of shock by extending the breakdown of the union beyond generic expectations.[10] The usual case in tragically resolved *nostos* plays is that either the one waiting kills the one returning, or vice versa,[11] and of course this usually entails the two individuals actually meeting at some point, in accordance with the structure of the *nostos* plot.[12] Yet in the *Women of Trachis*, husband and wife in effect destroy one another without ever making direct contact.

With the entrance of Heracles, carried on a litter, the plot resumes its winding path, due to the fallibility of human perception and the slow revelation of the truth. At first, it is not clear whether or not Heracles is even alive still, as he enters in silence, in contrast to all previous descriptions of him as wild and raging (e.g. 749-806). This temporary, unexpected calm is created only to be shattered. Hyllus accidentally wakes his father, who cries out in agony and demands that Deianeira be brought to him so that he may kill her with his own hands. Hyllus tries to explain that Deianeira was inadvertently the cause of Heracles' death, but his explanations fall on deaf ears. It is the mention of the centaur Nessus (1141-2) that serves to turn Heracles in another direction, and with him the plot of the drama: for at this point, Deianeira's effacement from the play is complete. Heracles explains that he only now understands a prophecy which said he would only die at the hand of one already dead – a prophecy fulfilled by Nessus' posthumous revenge.

The final plot turn comes with Heracles' injunctions to his son Hyllus. Heracles orders his son to help him die and thereby obtain release from his physical suffering. Equally odious to Hyllus is the second order that he take Iole as his wife, so that no one outside of Heracles' family will 'possess' (in both a sexual and material sense) the object of his desire. This reversal unexpectedly returns us to the original premises of the play, in new formulations. The core of the play's action is the (re-)union of husband and wife, and the (re-)establishment of the family unit. Yet now it will not be Deianeira and Heracles that will form the family, nor even Iole and Heracles, but rather Iole and Hyllus. Further, in another dramatic twist, it is Heracles, who has shown little concern for his family and its stability (insofar as the introduction of Iole to the house can be seen as disrupting the *oikos'* functioning; see pp. 88-92 below), who in the end re-founds his family by this harsh request, and Deianeira, who was most concerned to maintain the unity of the *oikos*, who is effaced from the family. Thus, as with the reversals in the first half of the play, so too in the second such reversals are not so much a matter of changing conditions, or of new events occurring, as of changing human understanding and response to the facts.

Should we understand this return to the original premises of the play (i.e. the reunion of the family) itself as a sign of a unity of action? The return of the unified *oikos*, which represents an enduring belief in the social institution of marriage (on this, see pp. 71-2 below) does give us some thematic closure. Yet on the level of the characters the play makes no attempt to suggest a full, seamless return, but rather emphasises the discontinuities by the fact that Hyllus must be *forced* to recreate the family, with an emphasis on the odium of the task. Hence we might suggest that the play's shortcomings in the matter of formal or aesthetic unity emphasise the need for the social unity that the family itself represents. The rupture of the plot, itself the result of a fundamental rupture between members of the *oikos*, serves to dramatise, by negative example, the need for families in general to act as unifying structures.

If the plot of the play is structured around shifting views of events in the play, this is also true of its frequent references to events that occurred prior to the action of the drama. These flashbacks typically involve reassessments of what has already occurred, in a pattern laid out early on by Deianeira when discussing how Heracles rescued her from the river god Achelous (26-9):

> But Zeus of contests brought about a good conclusion –
> if in fact it was good. For since being joined with Heracles

as his chosen mate, I continually nourish one fear after another
in my worry for him.

So too, Deianeira must reassess the centaur Nessus' gift of his
blood as a 'love-charm', and Heracles the past oracles he thought
he already understood.[13] Thus actions completed in the distant
past become present-time dramatic events because they must be
reinterpreted in the light of new knowledge. In this way the play
incorporates a static past into its dramatic present.

The *Women of Trachis'* most consistent quality in its dramatisation of the basic *nostos* story line is thus its frequent
changes in outlook and tone. This is not achieved primarily by
dramatising a succession of many different events, but rather
by presenting a succession of different (and often highly contradictory) interpretations and understandings of a limited range
of events, all of which is driven by a fundamental limitation in
the characters' knowledge of the events that make up their
lives. Moreover, the poet is remarkably free and bold in his willingness to use discontinuity and rupture to create plot-effects,
the most noteworthy example being the rift between the first
and second sections of the play. Finally, such a forceful use of
discontinuity and rupture provides a countervailing view to the
more familiar account of Sophocles as the most 'balanced' of the
tragic poets.

# 4

# Character

## Characterisation in Athenian tragedy

Since Aristotle, it has been claimed that in ancient drama action is more important than character.[1] Certainly characterisation in Athenian tragedy does not show the sort of *idiosyncratic* characterisation that we have come to expect, say from Ibsen or the nineteenth-century novel. In Sophocles' plays different types and classes of individuals all tend to use the same elevated tragic diction and grammar. The Nurse, although her 'lowborn' status is emphasised (62-3), does not speak differently from the queen Deianeira (and indeed both speak in a poetic manner different from colloquial ancient Greek). In contrast, different character types and classes in the novels of Dickens do tend to be characterised by verbal distinctions. In general there is in Athenian tragedy no exploration of character purely or simply for the sake of bringing out the individual's nature in all its specificity.[2]

Yet if Athenian tragedy does not primarily attempt to paint the particularity of an individual, the obvious must be noted: a tragedy is made up of speeches which convey the opinions and dispositions of the characters that make them. There is in fact in Athenian tragedy very little direct physical action by modern standards (the more violent physical actions – murder, suicide, etc. – take place off stage as a general rule), but rather, as we have seen in the case of the *Women of Trachis*, an emphasis on the human response to events. Hence there is in Athenian tragedy an interest in the portrayal of the mental states of its characters. Note also that

45

much ancient literary criticism, in contrast to Aristotle, *did* emphasise character, but such character was again not defined in terms of personality.[3]

It is perhaps simpler and more accurate to say that there is a very close relationship between character and action in Athenian tragedy. It is certainly not the case that character is simply and directly manifested in a person's actions, since a character will often hide his or her 'true' character in a play (e.g. Clytemnestra's deception of Agamemnon in the *Agamemnon* of Aeschylus), and Athenian tragedies often turn precisely upon a rupture between motivation and its realisation in deed (as in the *Women of Trachis*). Rather, such depictions of deception and of the rupture between intention and act are themselves based upon the assumption that there *ought* to be a direct relationship between character and action. Whereas today there is more of an assumption that character is a matter of an innate inner disposition that retains its nature regardless of external action, in Greek culture there is more of a view that character is dependent upon external action to validate or even establish it. Although we tend to see character as that which causes an agent's action (character, as the source of motivation, is prior to the deed), we will see that the *Women of Trachis* presents character as the product of action. This accords with the tendency in ancient Greek society to understand the individual primarily in terms of her or his social standing and reputation.

These comments can only be suggestive of the sort of issues involved in thinking about the relation between character and action in Athenian tragedy, but one further point should be made. Certainly it is not enough to invoke the basic argument that there is no 'real' character that exists beneath the words and actions of a dramatic figure, and that thus there is nothing there to search out. Even if there is no 'real' character behind the words and actions of the dramatic persona,[4] this does not mean that we are not encouraged by the play to infer and construct this character. In fact, the general point should be made that this is quite similar to our everyday interactions with real people: character is always something we construct from externals, and is never directly accessible to us.[5] In terms of characterisation within a given play, the degree to which we are encouraged to do this depends on the particulars of the case in question, and with the *Women of Trachis* we are on stable ground, for the play continually directs our attention to questions of character and motivation. Most noteworthy is the question of Deianeira's decision to send the robe (the central event of the play), and whether she acts out of desire, self-interest or a sense of revenge. The play's emphasis on her change of mind in her response to the news about Iole certainly suggests a change in her 'psychological' state. Further, Hyllus in the second half of the play tells his father Heracles that his mother's motivation was completely other than it might seem ('this is the whole matter: she intended well but made a mistake', 1136). Another example is Lichas' false account of his master's attack on Oichalia, for this deception specifically raises the question of Heracles' motivation, since it makes this a question for the audience to consider, and not simply a given fact. The event remains the same (Heracles' destruction of Oichalia), but the motivation behind the deed is brought to the fore.

The *Women of Trachis* is thus a play that specifically encourages its audience to question the reasons, causes and motivations of the actions of its dramatic characters. Moreover our present-day response to the main characters is perhaps the single most influential factor in determining how we understand the play. This has been true of past scholarship, and is, I suspect, true for the modern reader new to the work: the play's vivid and contrasting presentation of Deianeira and Heracles, combined with our own highly character-driven sense of literature, practically guarantees that we will respond to the play in the first instance through our reactions to the characters themselves. Thus, provided that we do not unthinkingly apply modern concepts of character or individuality, the question of character in the *Women of Trachis* belongs at the forefront of our interpretation.

## Deianeira

Deianeira is characterised in the first instance by a certain passive and even powerless quality. As in the various accounts of the battle between Achelous and Heracles, she is always the passive bystander awaiting the result of others' actions (21-5):

> I couldn't tell you the course of the struggle,
> since I don't know it: if there was a spectator
> who was unafraid of the sight,
> he could tell you. For I sat struck with fear
> lest my beauty some day bring me pain.

Further, it has often been noted that Deianeira, at the opening of the play, has waited a long time before trying to discover what has become of her husband. This is an example of how a character's action can be motivated on more than one level, in that her slow movement to action (and only after being urged on by the Nurse, 52-7) suggests a disposition slow to act (and so can be understood as part of her characterisation), but also serves simply to begin the action of the play (and so can be understood as dramatically motivated). Her later initial decision to do nothing in response to Iole, and her subsequent (very hesitant) change of mind, strongly suggests the same passivity. As she says herself, 'I hate bold women' (583).

Another dominant characteristic is her sense of concern and anxiety, typically directed towards her family. Talking to the Chorus (148-50), she says that a young woman's life is happy

> until one is called a wife rather than maiden,
> and she takes her portion of anxieties in the night,
> fearing either for her husband or children.

Deianeira's fears for her family are often mentioned in the play, most often in relation to Heracles (e.g. 29-30, 49-51), as befits his present situation. The Chorus, after her suicide, describe her actions thus (841-4):

> This wretched woman, unafraid of such things
> and seeing great harm rushing
> upon the house due to the new union,
> herself applied the poison …

Thus the suggestion of 842-3 is that she is motivated by a desire to avoid harm to her home, harm which is said to derive from Heracles' affair with Iole. Despite her gladness at Heracles' success in 293-5, her concern for others more generally is shown in 298-302 where she expresses sympathy for the captives of Oichalia

> For a terrible pity came upon me, my friends,
> when I looked upon these wretched women,
> homeless in a strange land, with no country, lost,
> who before were perhaps born of free men,
> but now have a slave's life.

Similarly, Deianeira pities Iole because her beauty has led to her own family's destruction (462-5), just as beauty played a destructive role in Deianeira's life (24-5).[6]

This concern and sympathy for others is in keeping with another important characteristic, her ability to universalise her own situation and incorporate it into a general, or even philosophical, outlook, as her speech to the Chorus reveals (141-77).[7] Her sympathy for the captives of Oichalia, and her (initial) sympathy for Iole in particular, results in large part from an ability to identify with these other figures.[8] For Iole, as for Deianeira, the martial world of men has resulted in the breakdown of family ties. Iole is also like Deianeira in being a passive object of desire which has served to initiate violence. This self-reflective aspect of Deianeira's character is consistent in the play, as she is constantly reflecting back upon her own life and the lives of others. Such a reflective attitude is perhaps seen most clearly when she generalises about the power of *erôs* both to explain and to accept Heracles' actions in destroying Oichalia and bringing Iole to her home (438-49).

However, while Deianeira shows a sense of concern for the well-being of her husband, it is clear that she feels not only a

general sense of duty towards him, but physical desire as well.[9]
As the Chorus say (103-11),

> I hear that Deianeira, once eagerly sought,[10]
> with longing heart, like some pitiful bird,
> never puts to bed the longing of her eyes
> so that they become dry, but nourishing
> a mindful fear for her husband's journey,
> she ever wastes away on her anxious, widowed bed,
> awaiting an evil, grievous fate.

There is also strong imagery in her perspective on Iole's introduction into her home: 'Now being two we will await an
embrace under a single covering' (539-40). The Greek word
used for 'covering' (*khlaina*, a kind of cloak) denotes a garment
used in nuptial unions, specifically on the wedding night.[11] The
imagery thus clearly reveals a sense of sexual jealousy, as well
as the threat that Iole represents to Deianeira's position as
wife. Deianeira also unfavourably compares her fading beauty
with that of the youthful Iole ('I see the youth of one proceeding
as the other recedes', 547). All of this shows that Deianeira is
affected by sexual desire and sexual jealousy. Yet in her self-
reflective fashion, she notes that desire is all-powerful, and that
it 'rules even the gods as it wishes, and me as well' (443-4).
Hence her self-reflective nature, and her ability to generalise,
enables her to suffer the effects of sexual jealousy and yet not
condemn Heracles and Iole for their own sexual desire (compare
436-49). Since such attempts at generalising and at gaining an
objective account of things are typical of her character, her
view here of desire should not be understood as hypocritical or
deceptive.

While such characteristics as concern for family and
love/desire for her husband have often been used by scholars to
present an idealised picture of Deianeira's character, it is important not to ignore the element of self-interest in her character
as well. For her anxiety over the arrival of Iole is not simply
jealousy, nor simply a fear for her family in general, but also a
fear of what this new woman in the house will mean for

Deianeira's *own* position within the family. When the messenger first tells her who Iole is (just after Iole has entered the house, a symbolic movement that emphasises her intrusion into the *oikos*), he says (365-8):

> And now Lady, as you see, he returns and
> sends her to this home, not without thought,
> nor to be a slave. Don't think that.
> It doesn't make sense if he is heated with longing.

The precise details of Heracles' intentions concerning Iole are never given, but the implication is still clear: since Heracles is figuratively 'enslaved' to Iole, she will be no slave herself in the house. Whatever role is envisioned for her (and it is something more than only being a sexual partner, which function she could fulfil as a slave), she threatens to usurp Deianeira's own position within the family by replacing her.[12] In addition, the Chorus say of Iole that 'this new bride has given birth to a great Fury for this house' (893-5), while at 428 the Messenger says that he heard Lichas refer to Iole as a *damar*, a term in Greek that can be used of either wives or concubines.[13] Just as the messenger emphasises the fact that Iole has been sent to Heracles' home, so too Deianeira, who is not unaware of Heracles' other past sexual affairs (459-60), emphasises in her final decision to take action the fact of Iole's presence in the house (545-6):

> What woman could live together with this girl,
> sharing the same union?

While Heracles' relations with women in the past were perhaps upsetting and insulting, they were not a direct threat to Deianeira's own status and position within the family. It is specifically the introduction of Iole in some unclear but hardly servile status within the house that pushes the normally passive Deianeira to dangerous action. This ambiguous status is in part a result of the differences in rights between concubines in the world of epic myth and concubines of fifth-century

Athens. For by the general time the *Women of Trachis* was produced it was not possible for an Athenian to beget legitimate children by a concubine. In contrast, many noble heroes of myth were produced in just this way.[14] The threat is all the greater because Iole is herself, as the daughter of King Eurytus, of noble birth, and hence could usurp not only the sexual role of Deianeira but also her social status as the wife of Heracles (something that would be less likely if Iole had no social status deriving from her own family). Indeed, given that the later children of Iole and Hyllus were the Heracleidai, an illustrious and aristocratic family from whom the Spartans claimed descent, Iole *does* in this sense usurp Deianeira's role as the woman who perpetuates Heracles' family line.

Such self-interest is also revealed in Deianeira's typically aristocratic, but also more generally Greek, concern for her reputation. This is clear from the fact that she wishes to keep her use of magic hidden. Asking the Chorus to keep the plan a secret, she says (596-7):

Only let me be well concealed by you: for in darkness,
even if you do shameful things, you will never fall into shame.

Her sense of potential shame here derives from the generally negative view Greek society had of women who used magic to obtain their objectives. It can also be seen that her sense of jealousy towards Iole is bound up with this concern for reputation, as she notes that she is afraid 'lest Heracles be called my *husband*, but the younger woman's *man*' (550-1). Ironically it is her concern for reputation that leads her to shameful acts that threaten her reputation.

This description of Deianeira allows us to address the central action of the play, her sending of the robe to Heracles. While a few scholars have argued that Deianeira in the *Women of Trachis* hides her true motives and in fact kills Heracles on purpose, it is generally accepted that she made an error of judgement in allowing herself to believe the lies of the centaur Nessus when he said that his blood would act as a love charm.

## 4. Character

On this interpretation Deianeira can be reproached not so much on ethical grounds, but rather stands guilty of a certain degree of foolishness. As she says later (707-8), after seeing the woollen swab disintegrate, how could she have thought the centaur, who died because of her, would wish her well? However, it should be noted first that this view, which has Deianeira make a highly foolish decision, does not fit at all well with what we have seen of her reflective nature: indeed, seeing that she is given to questioning the feelings and motivations of others (Heracles, Iole), we might expect her to question the motivation of the centaur. Of course, this could be just the point, that the play presents a stark contrast between her reflective character on the one hand, and on the other her rash decision due to sexual jealousy and the threat of another woman in the house. However, Deianeira's hesitant movement towards adopting the plan of the robe does not itself suggest such a contrast, such a sudden plunge into irrational reaction.

A recent study by Christopher Faraone is helpful in addressing the question.[15] Faraone shows that within ancient Greek thought, a love charm could be understood precisely as a poison. Such a charm was often viewed as something that by causing desire necessarily weakened, and even emasculated, its victim. The key was to apply the drug in a controlled way such that a love charm did not cross over to become a deadly poison. According to this view, it can be suggested that Deianeira knows full well that Nessus' blood is a poison, as in fact the story suggests, given Heracles' use of the Hydra's blood on his arrows. However, this does not mean that she looks to kill Heracles by using it. Rather her mistake is to accept Nessus' account that it is a poison that can *also* act as a love charm. This understanding fits well with Deianeira's hesitation before using the blood: she knows there is risk involved, since she is using a poison, but hopes that it will work in its (professed) capacity as a love charm, if used in a limited fashion ('limited' here perhaps by virtue of being put on the robe, rather than given to Heracles to ingest). This seems to agree better with the picture of Deianeira as a reflective individual, for by this understanding she takes a calculated risk but fails to understand properly the degree of risk involved.

Yet this account, although it defends Deianeira against gross stupidity, also condemns her to a certain extent on an ethical level. First, even if the poison succeeded in winning Heracles back to her safe and sound, the use of magic remained something of a shameful activity. As we saw, Deianeira admits this herself in her desire to keep the matter hidden. Yet more importantly, the equation of love charm with poison suggests that Deianeira is willing to risk the well-being of Heracles in her attempt to win back his attentions and maintain her position in the family. This sense of risk is seen in her short debate with the Chorus over whether she should send the robe (584-94):

> *Deianeira*: But if I should somehow prevail over
> this girl with spells and charms against Heracles,
> the deed is prepared – unless I seem to be acting
> rashly in some way. And if I am, I will stop.
> *Chorus*: But if there is some ground for success
> in the doing, you do not seem to us to be planning badly.
> *De*: Well, there is ground for success in so far as
> I think it will work – but I have not tried it yet.
> *Ch*: But you must know when you act, since you
> can have no knowledge without testing it, even if you think
>    you have.
> *De*: We will know soon. For I see this man ...

Breaking off the discussion as Lichas approaches, Deianeira ignores the warning of the Chorus that she does not yet truly know the effects of the blood. Clearly she is willing to take the risk in her desire to win back Heracles.[16]

At this point another motivational question can be raised: just why does Deianeira use the cloak to try to win back Heracles' affection? Earlier generations of scholars were sometimes prone to romanticise her character and simply say that she acts out of 'love' for Heracles.[17] This is not so much simply wrong as it is misleading and reductive. As we have seen, the text does emphasise Deianeira's concern for the well-being of her husband and family. However, 'love' is not a good English translation of the Greek word *erôs*, and as we have also seen, physical desire is also a part of Deianeira's motivation. More recent scholarship has tended to emphasise what might be called the social realities of the situation, suggesting that we consider the pragmatic conditions that might have pertained for a woman in a situation like Deianeira's.[18] This in turn suggests that her motivation be understood as one of self-preservation: on such an account Deianeira simply acts to preserve her position in the *oikos*, which is being threatened by the arrival of Iole.

The unspoken assumption sometimes made here is that the interpreter must choose between these options: Deianeira is either motivated by desire and love, or is motivated by self-interested concern for the preservation of her position within the home. Hence Faraone, for instance, urges the view that Deianeira does not act out of desire, but from simple self-preservation.[19] Yet since the text presents Deianeira as motivated by concern and desire for Heracles as well as by anxiety over her status within the house after the arrival of Iole, the real source of difficulty here may not be the play or its characterisation of Deianeira, but the interpretative assumptions we make in trying to assess the figure. For the simple answer, since the play makes no issue of this multiple motivation, is that the two basic forces driving Deianeira's actions can be conflated or even equated: Deianeira shows concern and desire for Heracles simply *because* he is the source of her social and familial status as the hero's wife. On this account, self-interest and desire are one and the same. Such a conflation seems suggested by Deianeira's suicide, as narrated by the Nurse (905-22):

> And she wept, poor woman, whenever she touched
> any of the things she had used before.
> And rushing here and there in the house,
> if she saw the form of one of her dear attendants,
> the unhappy woman would weep as she stared at them,
> herself crying out at her own misfortune.
> And when she broke off these activities I saw
> her suddenly rush into the bedroom of Heracles,

(keeping out of sight I watched her)
and I saw the woman throw a cover over the bed of Heracles.
When she did this she threw herself into the middle of the bed,
and breaking out in a warm flow of tears said:
'My bed and bedchamber, farewell
now forever, as you will never again
receive me as a bed-partner in this bed.'

This passage, with its references to 'her own misfortune' and her household items (it should be recalled that Deianeira's position as wife of Heracles is not only one of status, but one also of wealth), suggests a sense of personal loss. Yet this loss is expressed through repeated references to the marriage bed, a symbolic object that incorporates a range of connotations, from reproduction to familial concern to sexual desire. In relation to this last point, we saw that the Chorus in the prologue specifically spoke of her not being able to put her longing 'to bed', and Deianeira herself spoke of her sharing her bed with Iole (both passages quoted above). Moreover, Deianeira's preparation of the marriage bed is an act that has overt sexual overtones, as this was traditionally what a wife would do before having sex with her husband.[20] Finally, given that she impales herself with a sword, the sexual dimension seems clear.[21]

The reason that we may feel the need to choose between self-interest on the one hand and love and desire on the other in understanding Deianeira's actions may be due to present-day assumptions that the two are in some fashion incompatible. If we think of *erôs* in terms of the modern English word 'love', then the conflict is obvious: according to modern conception love is often practically defined by a lack of self-interest, since love is often specifically 'proved' by self-sacrifice. Yet even with an emphasis on sexual desire, a similar notion of incompatibility can be suggested within some modern day preconceptions. For sexual desire is often understood as somehow primal, indeed as a sort of first cause or motivation that often does not need to be explained itself. And if desire is primal and originary, then there is no need to seek further for motivation. However, sexual desire and self-interest/preservation are not logical opposites and thus there is no reason why they cannot coexist. Moreover, in the Athenian fifth-century institution of marriage the two concerns did overlap. A woman was given to her future husband, as noted, for the sake of producing heirs for the husband's family, a self-interested act to be sure. Yet there was still supposed to be, at least ideally and at the very least on the part of the man, a real sense of sexual desire, and even mutual affection.[22]

Moreover, there is a model of desire that explains quite well this overlapping of desire and self-interest in the character of Deianeira in the *Women of Trachis*. Desire can be understood as 'a desire of a desire' (also termed 'triangulated desire'),[23] meaning that we do not want something or someone directly (which would instead represent simple need), but rather we desire that which we think someone *else* desires. On this account, an object or a person can be desirable exactly to the extent that we believe that others desire this same object or person. The reason why this model works well to explain how Deianeira can be motivated both by sexual desire and by self-preservation is because, in keeping with the aristocratic ideals that are assumed by the mythical and heroic world of the play, for Deianeira self-preservation should be understood first and foremost as the preservation of her *reputation*. Since Deianeira, after her mistake is revealed, kills herself, it is clear that her first concern is not the preservation of life and limb, but of her perception in the world by others. It is a concern for her reputation that most occupies her in her final decision to use the robe or not, as her injunctions to the Chorus to keep the plan a secret show; so too does her comment after she sees the woollen swab with which she anointed the robe disintegrate (719-22):

> However if that man falls, I have resolved
> to die also together in the same onrush.
> For her who wishes greatly not to be base,
> it is unbearable to live with a base reputation.

Again, in the aristocratic world of appearance and social image, the reputation of a person, in an important way, *is* that person.

Deianeira's concern for reputation, together with the concept of triangulated desire, makes it possible to see how desire and self-preservation are linked. Deianeira's reputation comes first and foremost from the fact that she is the wife of Heracles. Hence her desire, in keeping with the very social and public world she inhabits, may be understood as 'a desire of a desire': others esteem Heracles in the highest terms for his labours ('the best of men', 176-7, 810-11; compare also 193-9), and so Deianeira desires Heracles for this social reputation which is in turn imparted to her and her family by her association with him as his wife. As she says when she learns that Heracles is returning home after his destruction of Oichalia (293-5):

> How could I not rejoice with fully justifiable feeling
> upon hearing of this successful deed of my husband?
> There is a great compulsion for my feeling to match his deed.

Note that she says this despite her sympathy for the captives of Oichalia.

Moreover, there are some indications that Heracles' desire for Iole is shameful because he has been mastered by his desire. Lichas took pains to argue (250-1) that Heracles' literal enslavement to Omphale was not shameful since Zeus was the cause (thereby suggesting that normally this would indeed be a shameful fact, just as it suggests again that Deianeira is in fact concerned with issues of reputation), and yet the play continually describes Heracles himself as figuratively enslaved to Iole (e.g. 365-8, 488-9). Certainly, Heracles' specific action due to his 'slavery' (the destruction of a city) is hardly presented in a positive light. In all of this the key point is that Heracles can be viewed as shameful for his lack of self-restraint (see pp. 88-9 below).[24] Hence Deianeira's attempt to win Heracles back can also be understood as an attempt to save the reputation of her family from Heracles' actions (compare again 'great harm rushing upon the house due to the new union', 842-3). Also, note that she does not, like other tragic heroines (such as Aeschylus' Clytemnestra in the *Agamemnon*, or

Euripides' Iphigenia in the *Iphigenia in Aulis*), seek fame in her own name.[25]

Hence, in that typically Greek cluster of ideas which defines women in terms of procreation and sexual desire, this desire for Heracles as a socially esteemed figure is in turn presented as a *physical* desire. Such a translation of desire from one level to another is not here surprising, given that it is Deianeira's sexual role in her relationship with Heracles that has gained her status as Heracles' wife, since again, procreation was the first purpose of marriage. In this regard, an interesting point to note is that Deianeira in fact assumes that Iole *herself* feels desire for Heracles (443-4):

> For he [Eros] rules even the gods as he wishes,
> and indeed me as well; why not another woman like me?

Victoria Wohl suggests, in drawing attention to this important point, that Deianeira attributes to Iole a desire for Heracles in order to try to exonerate her own (ultimately destructive) desire for Heracles.[26] However, we can argue that Deianeira simply assumes Iole's desire for Heracles because Heracles' status make him a suitable object of desire.

Kirk Ormand has given a good account of how Heracles in his relations with women operates upon what can be termed a homosocial level:[27] that is, his actions in relation to women tend to reflect a contest between *males* for recognition and social power, with the woman acting as a marker or sign of prestige. On this account, Heracles originally claimed Deianeira as his wife as a means to fame by overcoming the (hyper-)masculine figure of Achelous. So too with his destruction of Eurytus and his city for the sake of Iole: Iole is not simply desired for herself, but also as a sort of material prize and sign of Heracles' defeat of a male rival, Eurytus (compare 254-62, where Heracles is said to have sworn vengeance on Eurytus for – indirectly – causing his servitude to Omphale). In contrast, Ormand suggests that Deianeira attempts to be the direct object of Heracles' desire, and not just a marker for Heracles' desire for prestige within the eyes of other men, and that this is her tragedy: she never recognises that she is not a direct object of Heracles' desire, but merely a token of his homosocial desire. Yet if, as I have argued here, Deianeira's desire for Heracles is itself a desire for public recognition, then for Deianeira Heracles also represents an 'object' of desire. If Deianeira (and later Iole) is a mark of prestige for Heracles, so too is Heracles the object that gives social recognition to Deianeira. In this regard, Deianeira and Heracles are quite similar, both being clearly 'heroic' in their focus upon their reputations.

## Heracles

The character of Heracles is structured in good part by two oppositions. The first is between his role as a force for civilisation and his role as a force of primitive bestiality that often disrupts civilisation. The second is between his life as a mortal on the one hand, and his later existence as a cult hero and a god on the other.

No matter how unpleasant the picture of Heracles in the second part of the play may be at times to the modern reader, it is important to understand that his positive aspects are also emphasised. As noted, he is repeatedly referred to as 'the best of men', and this clearly refers to his labours, which were believed to have cleared the world of the monsters that had previously inhabited it.[28] Heracles himself speaks of having 'cleansed' the world (1061) by destroying these savage creatures, even suggesting the debt that the Greeks thereby owe him (1010-13):

> Where are you,
> you most unjust men of all the Greeks, for whom,
> cleaning out so many things on the sea and throughout every wood,
> I wretchedly destroyed myself ...

This theme of Heracles as a force for civilisation is emphasised in fact from the very beginning of the play; Deianeira's opening tale of how Heracles rescued her from a bestial union with a primitive river god (6-25) presents him as a bulwark of society's institutions. For the ancient Greeks, who were raised on stories of Heracles' labours, such references would have been sufficient to remind them of his positive aspects.[29]

Yet the play also undermines these positive aspects of the figure, by presenting Heracles as a primitive force that *threatens* the works of civilisation.[30] Most noteworthy here is his sack of Oichalia. For quite unlike Heracles' other exploits, which could be understood to have a civilising effect, the sack of Oichalia is the exact opposite. Of Heracles the messenger says (359-62):

> But when he did not persuade the father to
> hand over the girl so that he might have her as a secret partner,
> having first prepared a slight accusation and cause,
> he made war against her country ...

Thus while Heracles' desire for Deianeira in the past led to the destruction of a bestial river god, his desire for Iole leads to the destruction of a city, a clear symbol of human civilisation. Further, while his victory over Achelous led to a proper union between man and wife, the sack of Oichalia plays a key role in the breakdown of his own family, and the family, like the city, is another fundamental institution of civilisation. Indeed, given that the civilising function of the family is in large part due to its ability to regulate sex and procreation, it can be seen that Heracles' unregulated desire for Iole undermines the civilising function of the family in a blatant fashion.

This opposition between civilisation and bestiality is inherent in the mythical figure of Heracles. For while it may seem odd that such a savage figure could be understood as a civilising force, this is reflective of a characteristic aspect of Greek thought, namely that like should counteract like. For example, a murderer could be 'cleansed' of his crime by washing his hands in the blood of a sacrificial animal victim. Similarly, Heracles must be a violent force in order, paradoxically, to carry out his civilising function. This thought pattern is evident in the play in a reverse sense as well, in that the savage Heracles is ultimately only defeated by these same savage creatures (the centaur Nessus, the poisonous hydra).[31] Moreover, the idea that violence may lead to civilisation returns at the end of the play, and in a manner appropriate to the character of Heracles. Just as his desire for Iole destroys his family, in large part because it defies the regulating function of the family as a civilising institution, so too does this desire ultimately recreate his family. Of course, this is done in a typically direct and violent fashion – by forcing Hyllus to accede to his wish that he marry Iole. It is his savage nature that will lead to a civilising function, for it is precisely his desire to somehow keep Iole as the object of his passion that leads to this new union between Hyllus and Iole. Thus at the end of the play the figure of Heracles functions in a fashion largely consistent with his portrayal throughout the play, and in agreement with an important aspect of his general mythological nature, namely as a savage force that ultimately produces civilising results.

Thus we are encouraged to take a balanced view in the matter of Heracles' primitive nature. First, there is no doubt that the play emphasises the negative part of the contrast between civilisation and bestiality, since all of Heracles' productive endeavours on behalf of humankind are presented in the play as being in the *past*. In the present-time of the play, he functions primarily as a destructive force. Yet, as we have seen, Heracles' violent refashioning of his family at the end of the play recalls his role as a force for civilisation. Moreover, it should be emphasised that his civilising function does not somehow make up for his violent nature; it is not a matter of balancing good with bad. Rather, the play shows how the civilising aspect of Heracles only comes about *because of* his violent nature, that the positive aspect is dependent on the negative. Indeed, this is clear in his refashioning of his *oikos*. For his jealous desire for Iole which causes the family to be renewed is only the replaying of his original 'rescue' of Deianeira from the river god Achelous. For it is clear, from the various accounts of this battle, that at that time he was primarily motivated by sexual desire for Deianeira.

The other opposition in the mythic figure of Heracles is that between his humanity on the one hand and his later existence as a cult-hero and god on the other. A cult-hero was someone, typically born of a human and a god, who died and became an underworld *daimôn*. This *daimôn* was a sort of primitive spirit (not a god) which was closely attached to certain sites where the hero was understood to be buried and where the hero could be prayed to for concrete aid. Cult-heroes were often 'larger than life' figures (as clearly Heracles himself is). But in so transcending human limitations, a Greek hero was not necessarily 'better' than the rest of humanity, but simply more powerful. In particular, a Greek hero need not be morally or ethically superior to other humans, just as the Greek gods were often not morally or ethically superior to mortals. Indeed, a Greek hero need not even be particularly 'likeable' (perhaps even for the ancient Greeks themselves), a simple point that is highly relevant to the *Women of Trachis*; many less than enthusiastic receptions of the play have much to do with a distaste for the character of Heracles. Heracles was an important cult-hero at Athens, as evidenced by the fact that there were more cults for Heracles in Attica than for Theseus, the 'national' hero of Athens.[32] Finally, note that Heracles, in addition to his posthumous status as a hero, was also worshipped as a god.[33]

It should be understood that the dichotomies savage/civilising and human/divine do not simply overlap. Heracles' savage nature is not simply a result of his humanity any more than his civilising function is a result of his being destined for heroisation and deification. Religiously, a mortal was understood to be a being that existed on a level between beasts and gods. However, so long as we do not relate the two sets of oppositions in a simplified fashion, there are some parallels in how they are used in the play. For Heracles' generally divine or otherworldly nature is generally outside the action of the play, in the future, just as his civilising aspect was primarily to be found in the past.[34] This is most clearly seen from the fact that the play does not actually present or even explicitly refer to the apotheosis (deification) of Heracles (see below, pp. 108-13). Equally important is how Heracles, for all his great strength, is continually presented in the play as all too human in his fallibilities. Although Heracles becomes calmer with the realisation that the oracles he received earlier have turned out to be accurate (1143ff.), his original misunderstanding of the oracles is highly representative of his humanity, since such misunderstanding is typical of the divide between the divine and the human worlds. Further, the most powerful of figures, Heracles, has been brought low by a woman, as emphasised at the end of the play (1035-40, 1048-52, 1062-3). Indeed, Heracles is himself 'feminised' by his suffering (1070-5):

> Come, son, bear up, pity me who am
> piteous to many, crying and weeping
> like a maiden. No one could say
> he ever saw this man acting like this before,
> but I always attended my troubles without a groan.
> But now in my misery I am discovered a woman.

Moreover, the way in which he refers to the unveiling of his wounds ('I will reveal these [sc. wounds] from under their coverings [*kalummata*]', 1078) bitterly suggests a bride's *anakaluptêria*, a marriage ritual whereby she lifted her veil (*kalumma*) and revealed herself to her husband.[35]

It is an open question whether the end of the play returns to Heracles' otherworldly or divine aspect, just as it recalls his civilising function. As noted, Heracles does seem to calm somewhat when he learns the truth of the oracles, and this, combined with his sudden instructions to Hyllus to burn him on the pyre, may suggest that he sees beyond the present, that he himself has gained some sort of prophetic knowledge. On the other hand, he seems to accept that he is going to his death and nothing more, as his desire to be freed of his pain by dying shows (e.g. 1208-9). Yet at least in one respect he does regain his heroic, larger than life, status, and this is in the matter of his ability to endure his pain and suffering. His strength, once he learns the truth of the oracles, is turned inward, as he is able to master his pain and even to 'conquer' it by committing himself to the flames of his funeral pyre. Such a towering act of violent self-destruction leads us from Heracles the suffering mortal to a suggestion of the otherworldly force he is soon to become.

Thus Heracles' presentation in the play as a human on the verge of becoming something else, something otherworldly,[36] along with his dual status as a civilising and a bestial force, makes for a highly ambiguous figure. It is not a matter of freeing the character from criticism. As a human agent he is certainly an upsetting and ugly figure. Nor is such a critical view of his character anachronistic, since Heracles is often in conflict with fundamental Greek values. As discussed above (p. 23), a Greek was supposed to strive to aid and help his family and friends, a value which Heracles disrespects by his elevation of Iole and belittling of Deianeira, and by his commands to Hyllus.[37] If anyone within the action of the play upsets this value by not maintaining those reciprocal obligations and duties, it is certainly Heracles and no other. However, a critique of Heracles as a husband and father cannot be the final word, because he is clearly also something more than a human agent. The very fact that Heracles does not fit easily into a single category – beast, human, hero, god – reveals the interpretative difficulty involved, since it is in part by such straightforward categories that we form judgements about characters. The play does not invite the audience to simply say 'Heracles has transgressed basic social bonds, and so must be condemned' any more than it invites them to say 'Heracles is superhuman/ divine, and so cannot be judged by human standards'. Lying beneath the question of how we should respond to Heracles, for both ancient and modern audiences, is the more fundamental question: 'What is Heracles?'

Finally, Deianeira and Heracles exemplify the kind of characterisation by opposites that is typical of the extant work of Sophocles. Antigone and Creon in the *Antigone*, Odysseus and Philoctetes in the *Philoctetes*, Ajax and Odysseus in the *Ajax*, all acquire dramatic force through sharp relief and

direct opposition, often aligned along a whole range of
thematic differences (religious outlook, conceptions of
nobility, etc.). In addition to the disjunction between them
that is generated by the extreme dramatic separation of the
twofold plot which never allows the characters to meet on
stage (like the *Ajax*), the contrast between Deianeira and
Heracles is also emphasised by their gender difference (as in
*Antigone*). Heracles is the paradigmatic 'man of action', while
Deianeira is passive and slow to act. Deianeira's thoughts are
continually focused upon others (Heracles himself, her family,
society as a whole or even posterity), while Heracles tends to
see things only from his own position. Finally, Heracles'
complex status as beast, man, hero and potential god is in
sharp contrast to Deianeira, who is consistently presented in
her fallible humanity.

Yet the two characters, while obviously presented in a
fashion that emphasises their differences, are not simply
diametrical opposites. While some of the contrasts just listed
reflect fairly common fifth-century ideological conceptions of
the differences between the genders, the two figures are not
simply paradigmatic examples of 'Man' and 'Woman'. The
self-reflective aspect of Deianeira and the unrestrained sexual
appetite of Heracles present an emphatic reversal of fifth-
century conceptions of the genders. For it was typically the
woman who was thought to be excessive in her appetites,
including sexual appetites.[38] The Greek virtue of *sôphrosunê*,
a term that has a range of meanings, including sexual
restraint, deference, moderation, self-control and self-knowl-
edge, was seen as most important for women, precisely
because they were assumed to be more prone than men to
sexual excess, immodesty, and generally uncontrolled behaviour. It was the man who was presumed to be more restrained
and controlled in his actions. Here the marriage terminology
suggesting the necessity of 'domesticating' the woman should
be recalled (see pp. 19-20 above). Yet in the *Women of Trachis*
the opposite is the case. Deianeira's passivity, but also her self-
reflection and her self-restraint, result in a character who

does all in her power to resist responding in an emotional and violent manner to the introduction of Iole into her home. Rather it is Heracles who is constantly portrayed in the play as unable to check his appetites. Another important reversal of roles lies in the manner in which Deianeira kills herself. Typically in Athenian tragedy, a heroine commits suicide by hanging herself. Deianeira's use of a sword calls to mind the military world of men, but also, given the play's emphasis on the sexual and the fact that she kills herself over her marriage-bed, the role of the penetrator in the sexual act. This gender reversal is symmetrical with the way in which Heracles is feminised by the robe's effect upon him.[39] Furthermore, Deianeira's active nature in this regard is in sharp contrast to Heracles at the end of the play, who is able to kill neither Deianeira nor even himself.

These reversals are important for understanding the play's potential criticism of gender norms – a matter I will discuss further below. For now I would suggest that the overall presentation of the two characters, especially the way they help to define each other as man and woman and yet also reverse some of the standard characteristics that were thought to define the two genders, illustrates the degree of particularisation that occurs at the level of character in Athenian tragedy. To the extent that Heracles and Deianeira embody certain standard assumptions of what a man was and what a woman was, (e.g. men = active, public; women = passive, secretive), the figures are not characters in the modern sense of psychological character-studies, but character-types (or simply ideological types). Yet to the extent that these standards of gender presentation are upset and even reversed, these characters are also individuated in a significant fashion. This is not idiosyncratic characterisation, since even the reversal of a character type still works with stereotypes of the genders (since it simply reverses the familiar oppositions); nonetheless, the dramatic figure is not simply representative of a whole group, but reflects both a particular set of circumstances and a particular character or nature.

## Hyllus

The character of Hyllus is constructed primarily by his inter-
mediary position between Deianeira and Heracles. His actions
and responses are at all times defined by his proximity to one of
his parents. Hence his initial condemnation of Deianeira after
seeing Heracles' suffering (734-7) is overturned by the realisation that she acted without malice, and so at this point he comes
to his mother's defence (1114ff.).

Easterling has therefore suggested that Hyllus serves as a
link between the two sections of the play.[40] This is true in so
far as Hyllus represents the only real continuity in the course
of the play in terms of the characters themselves. However,
the role of Hyllus does not so much unite the two parts of the
play, as emphasise once again the fundamental breakdown
that has occurred within the social order, within the family. A
combination of dramatic structure and the socially symbolic
helps to make this clearly and forcefully felt. Hyllus, as the
oldest son of Deianeira and Heracles, is a living symbol of
their union. He is the very purpose of their social bond, as he
is the heir of the house, and so the (envisioned) guarantee of
its survival and continuation. So, to have him serve as the
agent who relates the death of one marriage partner to the
other (739-40, 1130) emphasises by contrast the breakdown of
the family. The effect is increased if we consider that to each
spouse can be attributed the death of the other. Thus while
Hyllus serves as a structural link in the play, symbolically and
thematically his role highlights the rupture and breakdown
within the family.

Yet if Hyllus reflects the failure of the union and, at the
very end of the play, the re-establishment of a new marriage
union that will preserve the *oikos*, he does not simply share
equally in both parents. Rather, his is a coming of age story.[41]
Whereas he begins the play more fully within the world of his
mother, he must, by the end of the play, accede to the demands
of his father. As Heracles cruelly puts it (1064-9):

68

## 4. Character

Son, be a true-born child of mine and
do not value higher the name of the mother.
Give your mother to me, bringing her yourself from the house
with your hands into my hands, so that
I may see clearly whether you are upset more at my pain
than at hers when seeing her justly harmed and mistreated.

By ultimately acceding to Heracles' demands Hyllus makes his full entry into adult life, in particular because he takes up responsibility for the *oikos* and its survival, even if this means marriage to a woman whom he sees as responsible for his parents' death. This change in Hyllus is not a change in his personality (i.e. he does not undergo a psychological change), but rather a change in his social status due to external forces.

This transition is marked by two features, obedience to the father and acceptance of the rules or strictures of society – two things that are closely related. Heracles asks Hyllus to aid him, 'understanding that obedience to the father is the finest custom/law' (1177-8). Yet Heracles, knowing that he will soon be asking Hyllus to do the unthinkable, does not leave it at that, but cements this general notion of obedience to one's parents (a very strongly held cultural value among the Greeks) by exacting an oath from Hyllus to do as he requests (1181-90). The institution of the oath is of fundamental importance in a society largely without written contracts, since it acts as the guarantee for all sorts of social interactions, from commerce to political alliances. Thus when Hyllus eventually accedes (for the most part) to his father's demands, this marks his acceptance not just of the authority of his father in general, but of the rules of his society. Furthermore, the oath also suggests that Heracles is asking for more than a father would normally expect necessary.[42]

Yet if the character of Hyllus can be understood in terms of an integration into (male) society, it is again important not to reduce his character simply to a paradigmatic example of a rite of passage from childhood to adulthood. There is much in Hyllus' transition of a particular (and particularly unsettling) nature. First, Hyllus does not simply follow his father in the

69

succession of the generations that makes up the lasting structure of the *oikos*, but rather *replaces* his father, and in a very
overt fashion. Heracles himself makes this brutally clear
(1222-8):

> Once I am dead, if you wish to show respect, take
> this woman as your partner, being mindful of your paternal oath,
> and do not disobey your father.
> May no man other than you ever take this woman
> who lay by my side, but rather you yourself,
> boy, attend to this bed. Obey!

What is striking here is that Heracles' continuing sense of
sexual possession means that Hyllus will not simply take the
place of his father as the head of the family, but will have physical union with his father's mistress (and intended future wife?)
to produce this new incarnation of the family.[43] Yet Hyllus'
revulsion at this order is not related to sexual prohibitions, but
rather to ethical considerations. Hyllus is repulsed at the idea
that he must marry Iole because she is, to his mind, his enemy
(1233-7):

> Who would ever choose these things – she is
> the sole partner in blame for my mother dying
> and in turn for making you as you are – unless
> he were afflicted with avenging spirits? Better, father,
> that I also die, than dwell together with my greatest enemy.

Here we seem to have a recasting of the basic anxiety that the
wife is an 'outsider' to her new family, in that Iole is here
literally viewed as an enemy. Heracles' request is so counterin-
tuitive to Hyllus that Hyllus asks Heracles, in effect, to absolve
him of responsibility for this decision, and Heracles agrees
(1247-51).

Heracles' first demand of Hyllus is even more disturbing.
One of the worst crimes in Greek ethics was patricide, and this
is basically what Heracles asks of his son, as Hyllus himself
understands it: 'Ah, such things are you summoning me to,
father – to become your slayer and killer!' (1206-7). Again,

Heracles' request goes against fundamental cultural values. Here Hyllus avoids the full odium of the deed by a sort of technical loophole: he will not actually light the pyre that will end Heracles' life, but will see to all the preparations. Hence Hyllus' passage into the (male) social order and the re-establishment of the *oikos* of Heracles are only achieved by a transgression of the very values normally thought to maintain such institutions. Hyllus crosses an important interfamily division by sleeping with his father's partner and he re-forms his family by taking into the house someone he defines as an enemy. Finally, Hyllus brings about his elevation to the head of the household by ensuring the death of his own father.

Many scholars have thought that Hyllus' social transition calls for a psychoanalytic interpretation.[44] For quite like the familiar Freudian pattern, Hyllus, either partially or symbolically, kills his father and obtains his father's sexual partner (although Iole is of course not Hyllus' mother).[45] Yet drawing connections with psychoanalysis can also obscure the issue, for in contrast to Freud's theory, as popularly conceived, this conflict between the generations is not presented in the play as based on personal desire, since Hyllus is resistant to both of Heracles' demands. Rather, it is presented as a social necessity. The literal fashion in which Hyllus takes the place of his father can be understood as a forceful way of presenting the need for the (ephemeral) individual to be subsumed within the (enduring) social unit of the family. On this account, the play suggests that it is not the individuals who occupy the roles within the family who are important, but the roles themselves. 'The oikos is permanent, but its members are not.'[46] For the family to survive and continue, the individual is not as important as the role she plays within the structure of the family. For it is that structure that endures, even when, as in the case of the *oikos* of Heracles, the individuals of the family come to destroy one another. Hence the drama of Hyllus' coming-of-age story is not one of some personal, subjective desire structuring the family, but quite the opposite, one of personal desire being force to yield to the requirements of the social order, since

Hyllus will refashion his shattered family in spite of himself and his own feelings.

A general conclusion can be drawn. It was noted above that character in Athenian tragedy tends to be dependent upon action. Character in the *Women of Trachis* can now be seen further as dependent also upon the social roles that pre-exist the particular individuals who occupy them. The play specifically stages some of the ways that character is secondary to action and social formation, and does not simply assume it as a precondition of the genre. Hence the *Women of Trachis* suggests that the question to ask is not 'What conception of character should be employed to understand the actions of the characters?', but 'How do the events, actions and conditions of the play *form* character?'. For the *Women of Trachis* dramatises the ways in which character is constructed, whether by the power of *erôs* and the desire for reputation working upon Deianeira, or the force of social institutions working upon Hyllus, or even, in the case of Heracles, different forms of existence vying for dominance within a single being. In the *Women of Trachis* character is not a stable centre from which dramatic action and conflict are produced, but rather character is the play's unstable and unsettling product.

# 5

# Performance

In the past few decades of scholarship on Athenian tragedy, beginning with the highly influential work of Oliver Taplin, there has been a heightened interest in the performative and dramatic aspects of the genre. Before this questions of entrances and exits, acting, stage props, costumes and the like tended to receive less attention, both because the works today are primarily encountered as literary texts rather than as dramatic events, and because much of our knowledge of the manner and presentation of Athenian drama remains partial and speculative. Yet the fact remains that Athenian tragedy was a performed art, and if we have any interest in the historical nature of this genre, attention needs to be given to its performance aspects.

This interest has been accompanied by an increasing emphasis on the emotional aspect of experiencing an Athenian tragedy. Our knowledge of the original Athenian audience's responses and perhaps our own experiences of dramatic performance may suggest that watching a play is a more emotional experience than reading it. However, we should beware of simply privileging performance over reading: performance simply produces its emotional effects in *different* ways from reading. Certainly emotional effect is not restricted to or dependent upon performance. However, performance criticism's focus on emotional effect is a useful one simply because past scholarship has tended to emphasise the thematic content of a work rather than its emotional impact. Thus performance criticism can be employed to further investigate the emotional effect of Athenian tragedy.[1]

What follows is an examination of a particular sequence of scenes (presenting the central dramatic turn of the play), with a view to describing how they might have been most effectively presented in terms of their dramatic and emotional impact on an audience. Since our texts of the Athenian tragedies contain no stage directions, the comments that follow are necessarily speculative at times, but I hope they will give a sense of the range of possibilities that the *Women of Trachis* offers for emotionally engaging drama.[2]

The *parodos* of the Chorus (94-140) largely sets the tone for the play as a whole. Deianeira in the opening section of the play presents an almost uniformly negative view of her life. The Chorus respectfully reproach Deianeira for her pessimistic outlook. They emphasise that humankind's fate is always a changing one, and this means both changes for the better and changes for the worse. The images of Heracles tossed here and there upon the waves of the ocean, and of the whirling of the heavenly bodies, establish the mood as one of changing human expectations in the face of an unknown future. The choral dancing may have incorporated this sense of change and movement, perhaps in the form of highly contrasting gestures and positions (on choral dancing, see p. 26 above). It is tempting to suggest further that certain gestures and movements may have been repeated later within the different choral songs, thereby highlighting throughout the course of the play this sense of repetition in change.

As so often in the works of Sophocles, the optimistic mood of the Chorus will ultimately prove to be both accurate and inaccurate, since it will both reinforce the dominant mood of the play, and ironically contradict it. Of course, the play will ultimately support the Chorus' view that life for mortals is always changing, but the Chorus will also be shown to be incorrect in thinking that this means a change for the better in the case of Deianeira. Rather, Deianeira too is correct, in that things will in fact get worse. Yet at this precise moment, it is the positive aspect of the Choral ode that is taken up in the movement of the drama, as the Messenger enters and reports that Heracles is on his way home (180-3). Hence initially we have a happy reversal, just as the Chorus suggested could be the case, and this sense of joy is emphatically stressed in the text. Upon hearing the news, Deianeira calls upon the whole house to cry out in gladness at the news (202-4). The Chorus sings a song whose excitement is conveyed by its spontaneity (since it has not been prepared for by any exits or entrances, contrary to the usual dramatic practice) and its loose structure.[3] But the play quickly undermines and shatters this mood of joy. While the Chorus is finishing its song, another group of women enter, making for the largest gathering of characters in the extant dramas of Sophocles. These newcomers, captives from Oichalia, are contrasted with the Chorus both visually and audibly. As opposed to the well-born Chorus of women from Trachis (who, as companions of Deianeira, are presumably of similar social status), the captives were no doubt presented in appropriate costume, visually depicting their servile status. In contrast to the Chorus' happy dancing, the captives move in a slow, processional movement. Finally, in contrast to the Chorus' singing, the captives maintain their silence. Thus the (joyous) mood created by one group performance (the Chorus' song) is countered and overturned by another (doleful) mood created by another group performance (the silent entry of the captives of Oichalia). The obvious similarity between the two groups of women serves, by this parallel, to emphasise the important differences.[4]

Yet this contrast, since it is a contrast between two groups, remains a general one, and is not yet applicable to Deianeira. The play now moves from the general to the specific, dramatically fulfilling the reversal of her apparent good fortune. After hearing Lichas' largely false tale of Heracles' latest exploits, Deianeira's sympathy for the plight of the captives draws her closer to them. It can be suggested that as she asks Lichas about the identity of Iole, she physically moves towards her in her questioning. Further, it is likely that Iole's costume, mask, and perhaps position on stage were such that she could be visually recognised as someone particular or noteworthy among the larger group (see 377-9).[5] Hence the contrast between the two groups of women develops into a contrast between two women. Moreover, the contrast between Deianeira and Iole becomes a more pressing one, since Deianeira's reference to Eurytus ('Did Eurytus have a daughter?', 316) suggests that the silent figure she is addressing is Iole, daughter of Eurytus and Heracles' new mistress.

Thus the following staging can be suggested. The two groups remain separated, representing the basic contrast in their circumstances and conditions. Deianeira, standing closer to the Chorus (to whom she has just been speaking) slowly moves towards a particular individual among the captives who is made noticeable by her general appearance and costume. As she moves, the bridging of physical space is paralleled by her questions about the woman's identity, suggesting that she is 'coming closer' in both a physical and cognitive fashion, and that she will now learn who Iole is and what she means to Deianeira. Yet Iole remains silent and Deianeira breaks off her questioning and arrests her movement. The failure to obtain a response is, as David Seale mentions, arresting in itself, as 'silences are characteristically composed to be dramatically broken'.[6] Instead, Deianeira welcomes the captives into the palace, in a symbolic movement that indicates that a dangerous individual has been physically accepted into the house and so also socially accepted into the family.

The primary effect of the scene is to alert the audience to the importance of Iole and, by means of verbal clues such as line 316, to suggest her identity as the sexual object that will produce ruin in the house of Heracles, as the audience will have known from earlier accounts.[7] Further, with Deianeira's questioning and her possible movement on stage towards Iole, the scene raises tension as it suggests an approaching conflict between the women. Two factors suggest that the audience may have envisioned the possibility of a direct conflict on stage. First, Bacchylides 16 may reflect an earlier version of the myth that had Deianeira try to kill Iole (see pp. 32-4 above). Secondly, the scene may be patterned on the meeting of Clytemnestra and Cassandra (Agamemnon's war slave and concubine) in the *Agamemnon* of

Aeschylus, and there the wife does indeed kill the concubine due both to an affront to her status and to sexual jealousy.

However, with Deianeira's kind willingness not to press Iole to answer her questions, this potential conflict is deflected, since Iole is not yet revealed as the threat to Deianeira that she really is. Thus for a short moment the dramatic impetus of the play abates, since the audience is left for the moment without any strong clues as to how the issue of Iole will be resolved. However, with the captives' entry into the house, just as Deianeira is about to follow, the play takes another turn. This next reversal results from the dramatist's manipulation of generic convention, for the movement off stage of the captives of Oichalia, Iole, Lichas, and Deianeira raises the expectation that we will now have a formal choral song. Typically such a song will not in itself advance the plot, and so our expectation of a choral song increases the feeling that the play has reached a lull. Yet just as Deianeira is about to enter the palace herself, the Messenger speaks up and stops her, and by doing so reverses the direction of the play. Deianeira's departure would leave the matter of Iole unresolved, but the Messenger states openly that Lichas has lied, and that Heracles destroyed Oichalia out of lust for Iole, whom Deianeira has just unwittingly accepted into her home.

With Deianeira's emotional response to this news, the pace of the play again speeds up (375-9):

> Ah, wretched, where do I find myself now?
> What grief have I imported unknown
> into my home? So she was nameless, was she,
> as her escort swore, she who is so
> resplendent in looks and bearing?

The suggestion here is one of sexual jealousy ('resplendent in looks and bearing') and anxiety over Iole's status (the ironic 'so she was nameless', i.e. a social nobody) and hence her possible usurpation of Deianeira's position within the *oikos*. The emotional quality of this outburst, and the reasons for it, hint at the portrayal of Deianeira as the willing, vengeful murderer of

Heracles familiar from some earlier treatments of the myth. Yet just as this possibility raises its head, the action is again checked. Lichas returns, and Deianeira is unable to get him to confess the truth, so the Messenger takes over the questioning. The dramatic focus is now once again upon a silent figure, this time Deianeira herself. Earlier the audience waited for Iole to speak and were frustrated: here Deianeira does eventually speak, but her decision to do nothing about the arrival of Iole again frustrates audience expectations. For unlike the familiar vengeful figure from earlier myth, Deianeira's response maintains her characterisation as a woman marked by passivity and reflection.[8] She accepts that Heracles has had other women (459-62), and declares that desire is a force which rules over anyone as it wishes (441-4). But her reference to her past acceptance of Heracles' other sexual adventures only brings to mind the obvious difference between them and Iole: the other women were not brought back to Deianeira's home. This action is both an affront to Deianeira's feelings for Heracles and a threat to her own status within the home.

Deianeira's change of mind before and after the first *stasimon* (497-530) is portrayed through a carefully constructed and powerfully effective series of events. The construction of this reversal depends upon the hints and suggestions that the play arouses in the audience before her change of mind, and the dramatic effect is produced by the way in which these hints are realised. The most pressing question at this point in the drama is 'How will Deianeira respond?', which may be rephrased as 'Which potential Deianeira will emerge now that the crisis of the play has been reached?' As we saw, her initial emotional outburst suggests a passionate response more in keeping with the stereotype of the jealous wife. Yet in contrast to this we have the earlier portrayal of Deianeira in the play as passive and reflective, accepting and even philosophical about her misfortunes. It is this characterisation that initially wins out, when Deianeira with her dispassionate response to the news of Iole convinces Lichas to tell the truth.

As Deianeira goes off stage with Lichas, the potential for a violent response is still not ruled out. Deianeira's final mention of 'gifts in return for gifts' is an ominous reminder of the role of the robe in previous versions of the myth, and hence raises the possibility that Deianeira is being deceitful and will willingly kill her husband in revenge. These hints and anxieties are developed in the following choral ode on the power of Aphrodite, with its retelling of the battle between Heracles and Achelous. The song is both immediate and extended in its relevance. Heracles is described as having been motivated in his battle against Achelous by his physical desire for Deianeira. This makes Iole and Deianeira equivalent as the objects of desire of a violent Heracles, and so emphasises Deianeira's point that Heracles has always been driven by lust. To the audience this may suggest that Deianeira's acceptance of Iole is the 'right' choice: after all, if the two women have similar statuses by reason of the desire of Heracles, then perhaps Deianeira must simply accept Heracles' changing desire, now to her own disadvantage. Yet Deianeira's point about *erôs* was that it affects *everyone* as it wishes, including herself.[9] The Chorus reminds us of this with its opening line, since the mention of 'Aphrodite who always carries off the victory' (497) suggests that just as Heracles and Achelous found themselves mastered by the force of desire, so too will Deianeira herself, and thus also that her rationalistic acceptance of Iole into her home will ultimately be untenable. For Deianeira's attempt to respond in a dispassionate manner can be understood as an attempt to 'defeat' Aphrodite, something the ode suggests is not possible.[10]

Further, the ode at its end returns to Deianeira herself, shifting the focus from the obvious effects of *erôs* upon Heracles and Achelous to its less clear (at this point) effect upon Deianeira. Moreover, the final image of Deianeira at the battle reminds the audience of some of the stern realities involved for Deianeira in this erotic triangle (523-30):

And the fair, delicate maiden
sat far off on a hill,
awaiting her own husband.
(I speak as though a spectator)
Striven for on two sides,

the girl's visage awaits a piteous end,
and like an abandoned calf, is suddenly
separated from her mother.

The image of the lost young reminds the audience that Deianeira has left her birth family and is now dependent upon her new family with Heracles, and her position in this family is now threatened by the arrival of Iole. Perhaps most importantly, the end of the song turns away from Heracles' point of view to the viewpoint of Deianeira. We are reminded that she too is a thinking character, and not just a prize, and further, that she is a desiring subject, affected herself by *erôs* (see 103-11, 443-4).

When Deianeira returns on stage secretly and tells the Chorus of her plans to send the doctored robe, this sequence of scenes comes to a climax. Her emphasis on secrecy transforms the stage from a locus of open social interaction to one of hidden conspiracy. On the surface, this is awkward. Deianeira's discussion with a large group of women out of doors may strike us as anything but 'secret'. However, the ability of the Chorus in Athenian tragedy to operate as both group and character (focalised by the singularity of the Chorus leader, with whom Deianeira here converses) makes this transition smoother. Here, as a sort of minor character, the Chorus is asked for advice and is sworn to silence about Deianeira's actions. The effect of this scene on the audience might have been quite varied. On the one hand, the inclusive function of the Chorus may have drawn the audience in, making them feel as though they are included in the plan of Deianeira. On the other, as a group of women secretly planning, watched by a predominantly male audience, they presumably would have also activated male fears based on the ideological stereotype of the deceptive and destructive power of women (see pp. 19-20 above).

Deianeira's explanations for her new decision to act suggest that she is motivated both by sexual jealousy and a sense of personal threat. Hence the anxieties which the play has planted within the audience concerning Deianeira's response are here realised, and yet still in a novel fashion which does not simply have Deianeira revert to the stereotype of the jealous wife. Rather, since the element of deception was introduced by the centaur Nessus, Deianeira, who has no intention of destroying Heracles, is presented as consistent in her attempt to remain passive and self-controlled, and yet as ultimately overpowered by the power of *erôs* (540-6):[11]

> Such pay for housekeeping has Heracles,
> the one called loyal and noble,
> sent me in return for my long service.
> And while I do not know how to be angry at him,
> suffering so often as he does from this disease,
> what woman could live together with this girl,
> sharing the same union?

Thus her passive and self-reflective character is presented as overpowered by the circumstances that surround her. Further, this series of scenes, designed to delay the action and so to raise audience interest and anxiety, is carefully related to the charac terisation of Deianeira herself and her dramatically central choice. The resolution of this plot movement satisfies because it both matches and surprises the expectations that the play itself has raised: the introduction of Iole into the home of Heracles *will* be the catalyst for tragedy, but not on the familiar pattern. Deianeira, herself constrained by the force of *erôs*, will not remain able to resist the divine power that is so much emphasised in these sections of the play, and will indeed destroy her husband, yet she will not do so from a jealous attempt at vengeance, but from self-preservation and desire.

Thus this sequence of scenes gives maximum emphasis and dramatic weight to the anticipated meeting of Heracles and Deianeira (whether in marital reunion or tragic conflict) precisely by delaying it, thereby keeping unresolved exactly how this meeting should be envisioned. For the dramatic exploration of Deianeira's shifting response to Iole raises shifting expectations regarding the dramatic resolution of the *nostos* plot itself, so that we have character woven into action, and action woven into character. Interestingly, in a play that so much emphasises desire, the resulting plot-structure is one that produces a *frustration* of desire for the audience. For the play's build-up to the meeting of Deianeira and Heracles, a build-up produced by keeping the outcome of this meeting unclear for so long, is never resolved due to the simple fact that the characters never actually meet; on this level, the *nostos* plot is never resolved. And just as the characters never obtain their desire (Deianeira never regains Heracles, and Heracles must possess Iole only vicariously), a similar frustration of desire is produced within the audience itself, thereby revealing the truth of the statement that '*erôs* rules all' in an all-embracing manner that goes well beyond the scope of the Chorus' conception of *erôs*. The play's reversal of audience expectation not only produces exciting drama, but it also serves to engage the audience in the very emotions that constitute the play's thematic core.

# 6

# Theme

## Sex, family and gender

By focussing on the disruption of the family due to infidelity and sexual jealousy, the *Women of Trachis* raises questions about the role of the genders within the family and within ancient Greek society more generally. However, when considering how any artistic work can be used to investigate questions of gender and society, it is important to keep in mind the context and framework of these works, to take account of the filters, so to speak, which need to be used in evaluating any artistic work. For instance, no matter how sympathetic a modern audience may find the figure of Deianeira, it should be kept in mind that she is a literary creation of a male poet in a male-dominated society, and so is in part a construction of male ideology. This clearly poses problems for feminist scholarship within Classics generally.[1] Yet we should not assume from the outset that such works are incapable of critiquing the gender norms in which they are grounded. While it would be naive to start with the *assumption* that either Sophocles or his male audience held the status of women in their society to be something that required correction or improvement, this does not mean that an intelligent observer of the day could not recognise the possible problems that might result from a rigidly hierarchical social system that privileged one gender over the other. Moreover, regardless of the views of either poet or audience, any social belief or ideology will contain its own inconsistencies. Since ideology is an unacknowledged set of beliefs about 'the way things are', as opposed to an accurate representation of reality, there will inevitably be moments where such ideologies are unable to explain why things happen as they do. Ideologies can and do break down, and our texts suggest that Athenian tragedy either wilfully explored these failures, or at the very least gave a social space for such failures to be expressed in a relatively unthreatening fashion. In classical Athens the theatre served as a forum for the discussion of potentially sensitive subjects in a safe environment. A tragedy, with its distant, mythological figures, and often non-Athenian settings, could use this foreign or alien aspect precisely to raise questions about contemporary Athens: 'fiction' could serve as a means to make uncomfortable questions about present day realities more acceptable. This aspect of drama, which might be called 'contained criticism', is observable in its treatment both of contemporary politics, and, as in the *Women of Trachis*, contemporary social institutions, such as marriage and the roles of the genders within it.[2]

Since the characters in a tragedy are both constructs of the poet who created them and mythological figures, we must resist simply viewing their actions as transparent examples of historical situations and conditions. However, even though the *Women of Trachis* does not document the material conditions of women in fifth-century Athens, every artistic work is still, in a sense, a historical record: for what the play does document is how certain people at a certain time thought about the issues that the play raises. Hence Deianeira is completely 'real' in the sense that she is a historical representation of Athenian male anxiety concerning the role of women within the family. In light of this anxiety the character of Deianeira is exceptional in the challenge and criticism that she represents to this social order.

Marriage involved two central anxieties for the Athenian male. First, there was the anxiety that the new addition to the family, an 'outsider' with her own loyalties to her natal family, would not prove loyal to her new husband's family. Secondly and related to the first, there was the fear of female infidelity, that the succession of the family through the generations would be upset by the birth of illegitimate children not born of the father. Any such unregulated procreation, seen by male ideology as resulting from the (perceived) excess of emotion and desire in women, could spell the end of the unity and coherence of the family, since it threatened to introduce further outsiders into the family as its heirs. Athenian tragedy is almost obsessive in its interest in and anxiety over these questions, as numerous plays by all three tragedians demonstrate. Yet a comparison of Deianeira with some other famous 'vengeful wives' can be useful for drawing out just how potentially threatening and upsetting such a character might have been to the fifth-century male Athenian audience members, not despite, but because of, her sympathetic portrayal.

As we have seen, the character of Deianeira is a complex one, neither a stereotype of the jealous wife nor a simpleton free from all blame except foolishness. It is precisely because she avoids these extremes that Deianeira presents such a threat. Figures such as Clytemnestra in Aeschylus' *Agamemnon*, and Medea in Euripides' *Medea*, are clearly meant to flout and transgress contemporary accepted norms and values. Clytemnestra takes up with Aegisthus, an enemy of the house of Agamemnon, and attempts to usurp the rule of Mycenae by killing Agamemnon, primarily in anger for his sacrifice of their daughter Iphigenia at Aulis, but also out of revenge for Agamemnon's infidelity. Here the link between family and politics is direct, as Clytemnestra's usurpation of power in the family is also a usurpation of political power. Medea, abandoned by her husband Jason for another woman, kills their children as a way to get revenge, an act which reflects the male anxiety that the wife might not be loyal to his family, since she kills Jason's heirs, the most important product of the marriage. We have seen that earlier versions of Deianeira quite likely presented just such a transgressive figure. However, these sorts of figures, by their very extreme nature, by their 'monstrous' aspect, are arguably *less* disturbing to the degree that they are fantastic and removed from historical reality.[3] The shock value of these figures, powerful as they are, serves to remove them from reality for the spectator.

Yet the point is not simply that Deianeira is presented in a resolutely human (and so generally believable) fashion. Rather, what is potentially threatening about Deianeira is the way that she is presented with ideologically typical female characteristics which are at the same time bound and checked by the institution of marriage. Indeed, not only does she largely act in what could be called an acceptable fashion, but it is she, the woman, who strives to maintain a unified family, and Heracles, the male, who threatens to complicate and fragment it. Thus Deianeira for the most part plays by the rules of contemporary gender ideology, and yet still proves to be a force destructive to the family.

Hence the difference between Deianeira and a Clytemnestra can be understood as follows. The monstrous vengeful wife is an ideological rationalisation (fantastic as it may be) for the restrictions that marriage places upon women. It is like saying, 'women are potentially like Clytemnestra (i.e. destructive to the husband and his family), so that we (Athenian males who run the state) are justified in promoting an institution (marriage) that checks or restricts the (often sexually) destructive aspects of women'. Literary figures such as the wrathful Clytemnestra or Medea can be interpreted as ultimately supporting patriarchal rule since such figures serve to justify both male ideological assumptions about women, and the restrictive measures designed to regulate or control women in their perceived excesses.

Yet if an excessive female figure such as Clytemnestra serves to justify the institution of marriage, a more restrained figure such as Deianeira may raise more troubling questions about that institution and its efficacy. For if a character who is *not* monstrous destroys her husband and her family, this suggests that the institution of marriage is not up to the task it is in part designed to perform. Deianeira is generally normative in other regards as well (e.g. her passive nature and her loyalty to her husband's family). We saw that Deianeira was portrayed as acting under the effects of erotic desire, to the point that she willingly risks her husband's life and unknowingly destroys her family. Greek ideology views intense erotic desire as typical of women, but the important point in the *Women of Trachis* is that this desire is directed towards the husband. Hence Deianeira's desire is presented within the play as precisely the kind of desire that should be effectively regulated by the institution of marriage: if, by male ideological standards, women were seen as overly emotional and over-sexed, and the bonds of marriage were meant to regulate this threat to orderly procreation, and if Deianeira's desire is 'properly' directed towards her husband, then the play suggests that the fault does not rest entirely with the woman.

However, Deianeira's character also includes certain *non-normative* traits. In particular, she was seen not to be simply passive, but in fact self-restrained (*sôphrosunê*), hence going against certain ideological expectations.[4] Such a trait can only serve to make Deianeira a more suitable wife. Her self-restraint, coupled with her reflective outlook, produced an initial response to the introduction of Iole very different from earlier mythic versions. Her subsequent response, with its attempt to use magic to bring Heracles back under her influence, can be seen as transgressive, since it attempts to reverse the standard Athenian balance of power between the sexes. Yet it is not easily condemned because it is directed towards maintaining the unity and coherence of the family.

Thus Deianeira can be seen as threatening to male ideological beliefs, not because she is a larger than life figure, a woman who exceeds all boundaries in her excessive nature, but because she produces destructive results similar to such fantastic figures without in fact being so extraordinary. She suggests the internal failure of the system, exemplifying the sort of internal inconsistency that is inherent in any ideology. The positive traits of Deianeira are all the more notable since they tend to be absent from Heracles and his own actions. Thus the play ultimately throws the question of desire and the family back upon the husband, since it is Heracles who is ultimately the truly excessive figure whose desire disrupts the proper functioning of the family. It is Heracles who lacks *sôphrosunê*. Again the issue can only be addressed in light of the way the two characters mutually define each other.

It is therefore reasonable to suggest that the *Women of Trachis* does present criticisms of the social order of the day, and of the relation between the genders. The play can be understood as suggesting that excessive sexual desire, so often assumed to be a problem arising from the wife, can also be present in the husband, and thus that the husband also is responsible for a degree of sexual restraint. Moreover, given that Heracles' lack of restraint ultimately leads to his destruction and the near destruction of his own family, the play may even suggest that there is a degree of faithfulness that the husband in turn owes to his wife (which of course is still in contrast with the absolute faithfulness expected of the wife).

In fifth-century Athens it was considered acceptable for a husband to have extramarital sexual relations with other women (as well as with younger men). In this regard Deianeira is again presented as being in line with the prevailing ideological outlook (438-40; 459-62):

> You're not talking to some base woman or one
> who does not understand that it is ever
> humankind's nature to delight in different things.
> ...
> What's so terrible to understand? That one man,
> Heracles, has had many other women?
> And yet none of them has ever had
> a harsh word or reproach from me.

While other comments suggest a feeling of sexual jealousy on Deianeira's part towards Iole (see pp. 49-52 above), in the past Deianeira has recognised and accepted that Heracles has had other women. Nor does she use Heracles' particular nature as the reason for her acceptance, instead philosophically suggesting that desire is a power to which all are subject, and that to resist its effects is futile. But what is unsaid here is as revealing as what is said: this universal power of desire to affect individuals operates as an explanation or even as an excuse for Heracles' behaviour, but it would not, by the cultural standards of the fifth century, serve to free Deianeira of blame if she should behave similarly, even though the force that affects Deianeira is the same as that which affects Heracles, sexual desire.

Deianeira is of course unable to maintain her usual passive acceptance this time, and she is fairly specific as to why (533-8):

> I have come out to you in secret to reveal those things
> I have devised with my own hands, and so that
> I might find pity from you for the sort of things I suffer.
> For I have received a girl – though I suppose
> she's no longer a maiden but one bedded –
> like a sailor takes on a cargo, merchandise harmful to my mind.

As we have seen, Iole's physical presence in her home constitutes a further threat and insult to Deianeira. Sexual exploits outside of the home are one matter, but introducing a mistress into the home, perhaps as some sort of second wife, is another, one which would erode Deianeira's own position within the family. This physical presence is evidently too much even for a passive, self-reflective, woman such as Deianeira to accept. It is important to note that Deianeira in this regard seems to again reflect cultural values of the time of the play's production, since our evidence suggests that the decision to introduce a concubine directly into the house was one that was generally frowned upon.[5]

Hence the play questions not extramarital sex by the husband, but extramarital sex that upsets the established roles of the family. Heracles' decision to bring Iole into his home can be criticised not simply because it upsets his wife, but because it upsets a passive, loyal wife who accepts her position within a patriarchal household. Of course, one could always argue that even under these circumstances Deianeira should never have attempted to win back Heracles in so risky a fashion. As we saw earlier, Deianeira is certainly not free of responsibility in the tragedy that affects her and her family. However, the play suggests that her response to Iole is an understandable one. Again, it is not merely the fact that she is a generally sympathetic figure to most modern readers, but the fact that she possesses a number of qualities as a wife that would have been appealing to her fifth-century male audience members, which allows the play to question Heracles' sexual role in the breakdown of the family.[6]

Of course, the Heracles of the *Women of Trachis* is hardly an Athenian Everyman, representing the sexual attitudes of males in fifth-century Athens in general. In this regard, the very different nature of the two principal characters, the very 'human' Deianeira and the mythic/heroic Heracles, provides different perspectives on the question of the role of desire and responsibility in the tragedy of the play. If we emphasise the particular, exceptional nature of Heracles as an individual, it could be said that his actions need not be taken as a criticism of excessive male desire within the bonds of marriage, since no man is so excessive in nature. However, since the play, by its very structure, tends to encourage the audience to view events from the vantage-point of the fairly realistically presented Deianeira, the issue can, and I suggest should, be viewed in direct relation to the sexual mores of the day. Men *did* sometimes introduce other women into the house as sexual partners, even if these acts were often looked down upon. However, the different viewpoints that the play offers by having two very different types as central characters allows the audience to assess the thematic material of the play in two ways. Thus the exceptional nature of Heracles, in particular when contrasted with Deianeira, can be understood as another means by which the play makes its criticism in a less upsetting fashion. For if the play's criticism of the marital order (the idea that both members of a marriage must show a sense of sexual responsibility) results only by employing a mythic figure famous for his excessive sexual desire, then this allows for the view that the criticism is limited to the mythic past of Heracles, and is not therefore applicable to fifth-century Athenian males in general. As we discussed before, Athenian tragedy is often able to make the social criticisms that it does by means of this sort of contained criticism.

## 6. Theme

It is also worth noting that the presentation of Heracles as transgressing the social values surrounding marriage, and generally failing to maintain his *oikos*, is fully in keeping with the larger myth. The entire story of Heracles revolves around punishment for an insult made against the institution of marriage. Heracles suffers his famous labours because of the sexual infidelity of his father, Zeus, for which Hera, in jealousy for this infidelity, plagues the son. Hera was, above all else, the goddess of marriage, and hence her anger can be understood as the emotional response of the personified representative of the institution of marriage, and therefore as a sign of social recognition of the value and importance of this bond. It is therefore not surprising that the play is critical of Heracles in this respect, given that the myth itself raises just these sorts of questions.

Finally, this interpretation of the play's presentation of marriage and gender fits well with our discussion of Hyllus' coming of age and the re-establishment of his *oikos* (discussed in Chapter 4). The play's negative portrayal of Heracles does not result solely from sympathy for Deianeira or as a concern with the status of women generally, but primarily from the perceived and actual importance of the family. If the structure of the family demands that Hyllus replace his father (here in an unusually direct manner) in order to ensure the family's survival, so too it demands that the individual members of the family perform in certain ways in order for the family to function properly and to recreate itself. The Greek institution of marriage clearly privileged men over women, but it defined the social roles of men as well as women, and by doing so dictated to each in large part, if not equally, how they should live. This is highly ironic for the male heads of families, since they are supposed to be in control of a social institution that at the same time defines their proper activities in the service of the re-creation of the *oikos* itself.

Thus while the play does not question the imbalance of power between the sexes, it does question the ideology of family and desire, posing or exposing areas where the ideology is inconsis-

91

tent. In particular, it suggests that, given the assumption that desire was universal in its influence, sexual restraint also needs to be 'universally' applied to men and women alike, and that a system of marriage that does not recognise this will contain the seeds of its own failure.[7] For the *Women of Trachis* remains exceptional in its presentation of female desire. Ultimately, although the underlying myth is founded upon the fear of excessive female desire, Deianeira's guilt in the events of the play is not simply to be attributed to such desire. Deianeira's desire is only one element, and not the most important one, in motivating her actions in the play. Her contribution to the tragedy is a willingness to risk the life of her husband in her attempt to keep the family unified in order to maintain her own position within it, without possessing a proper understanding of the degree of risk involved. The destructiveness of excessive desire in our play is not attributed, as so typically in Athenian tragedy, to the woman but to the man. Such a reversal of ideological expectations can only raise uncomfortable questions about the social order that is based upon such expectations. If the play does not simply criticise the ideological assumptions underlying Greek marriage unions and the role of sex within them, it does make these assumptions something to question and think about. And since ideology is made up of beliefs which resist being questioned precisely because they are taken as 'normal', as transparently accurate (and thus uncontested) accounts of 'the way things are', the *Women of Trachis* can be understood in this limited, but important, regard as socially critical and subversive. The play is not feminist in overt make-up or intent, but it presents its society in a hard, clear light that brings to consciousness the inconsistent (and so unjust) workings of the ideological systems that supported such a system.

## Late learning

Perhaps the most dominant theme of the *Women of Trachis* is the commonplace Greek notion that one should not count oneself happy (or count oneself anything) until one has died and life can offer no more upsets or reversals of fortune.[8] Deianeira begins the play with this standard piece of Greek wisdom, but puts a negative twist on it, saying that she *already* knows that her life is wretched: she does not need to come to the end of her life to be able to judge hers, for she already knows it to be a sorrowful one.[9]

Despite this psychological pre-emptive strike against life's vicissitudes, her tragedy and her family's will go beyond even her own pessimistic outlook. In expressing her anxieties, it seems clear that she already accepts that Heracles could meet a violent end (which would not be surprising, given the violent nature of the character), and that there may be no reunion of the family. She is not wrong about this. But her expectations are fulfilled in a manner she does *not* foresee. It is Deianeira herself, despite her knowledge and generally self-reflective nature, who will turn out to be the agent of Heracles' death. Further, the family will survive, but in a form that essentially erases her presence, by having the heir of the house continue the family with Heracles' concubine Iole, her sexual and social rival. Thus, while Hyllus is of course her son, and so his descendants are also hers, the play presents the resolution of the action as one in which Deianeira is replaced by Iole within the family.

The theme of late learning is emphasised in the play by the way in which all three main characters suffer from learning something too late for this knowledge to be of any use. Deianeira of course learns too late that the poison she has used upon Heracles has no effect as a love charm, and is only the means for the centaur Nessus to obtain his revenge ('Why ever, and for what, would the dying beast be well disposed to me, because of whom he was dying?', 707-8). Hyllus learns too late the truth of Deianeira's motivation in sending the robe: thinking that she sent it with the purpose of killing his father, he hastens her to her suicide with his curse and accusations ('The wretched boy learned/ that he had fixed this deed by his anger,/ learning too late from one of the house slaves/ that she had done these things involuntarily due to the influence of the beast', 932-5). Finally, Heracles fails to understand the oracles; in the case of the first oracle, he mistakenly thought that there was a choice between 'death' and the 'end of his labours', when they referred to the same thing, since 'the dead do not toil' (1173); in the case of the second, the illogicality of the premise, that someone dead would in turn kill him, implied safety, but in fact referred to the centaur's posthumous revenge ('Ah, now I know in what misfortune I stand', 1145).

Thus the theme of late learning in the play is a conspicuous one. However, the very familiarity of the sentiment can lead us to oversimplify its presence. For in this work the poet takes the familiar sentiment and develops it to the extent that it questions the value of human knowledge itself. The theme of late learning will, by the end of the play, be supplanted by the theme of the futility of human understanding.

Late learning implies its own opposite, suggesting at least the possibility of *timely* learning, understanding gained when it can be usefully applied. For any act of short-sightedness there is the hope of the opposite, of the ability to understand one's situation and respond knowingly in an advantageous way. Yet the play undermines such a view, since Deianeira's opening statement, that she possesses a sort of limited knowledge, is ultimately disproved. Deianeira in effect takes the view that one can circumvent humankind's limited knowledge by assuming the worst-case scenario. Her 'knowledge' is bought at the price of simply assuming the worst to be her lot. Yet ultimately her knowledge is unable to encompass the extent to which she can, and does, suffer.[10] She is right that her life is, and will continue to be, an unhappy one, but she is wrong in thinking that she has somehow exhausted the depth to which her sufferings can reach. Hence the play, by emphasising this sort of minimal degree of human knowledge right from the outset, only to prove even this wrong, suggests in a forceful way just how limited human knowledge is.

The play presents this negative view of human knowledge in two manners, both of which can be drawn from the opening lines and their reference to popular wisdom. First, there is the inherent irony of the notion itself: if you cannot know whether your life is happy or not until it is over, then presumably you will *never* know the nature of your own life. The Greek implies this, since Deianeira literally says '*you* cannot judge before *someone* dies whether a life is happy or not', suggesting that only others can assess a life, that ultimately only a posthumous judgement can be accurate. This also fits with the weight that the Greeks placed generally on the judgement of the group, rather than that of the individual. Secondly, the conventional wisdom here does not contrast true knowledge with ignorance, but *any* knowledge with the reality of the event. The saying effectively argues that knowledge is largely unsure or useless until the reality interposes itself and establishes the truth. And since death itself is for the individual final and all-encompassing, it is the event that establishes once and for all the character or nature of a life, by bringing it to an end, and thereby finally making it clear in all its aspects and fortune. These two views of the failure of knowledge can be brought together by suggesting that the *Women of Trachis* does not simply present the sorrow of late learning, but rather the inability of human language and thought to encompass or deal with the brute reality of the physical, immediate world. There is a pervasive contrast in Greek thought between word and deed, and the *Women of Trachis* presents a world where the power and violence of the deed renders impotent the understanding of the word.

This suggestion can be supported by some further considerations. First, we saw above that the plot is in large part, as is often the case in Athenian tragedy, a series of changing human responses rather than a series of changing actions or events. Yet the *Women of Trachis*, like other plays of Sophocles, constantly evokes and emphasises the physical and the violent, as is fully in keeping with Heracles himself as a figure of physical might. The play begins with Deianeira's account of the battle between Heracles and Achelous (6-25), and this story is repeated in the course of the play (497-530). There is also the forceful manner in which Deianeira commits suicide, by means of a sword, followed by the extended scene in which Heracles is consumed alive by the poison of the cloak, as he shrieks and laments his fate. The play's action ends with a procession to Mount Oeta where Heracles will be burned alive on a pyre. Finally, the entire plot revolves around physical desire, in particular the fact that Heracles sacks an entire city (putting to death the males and enslaving the females) in order to fulfil his sexual desire for a single woman.

In addition to the play's focus on the brute physicality of the world, we also have a constant emphasis on the failure of mortals to understand this world they live in in any useful way. Deianeira at first thinks that her marriage to Heracles was a happy event, as it saved her from the beast Achelous, but of course it only meant more anxieties for her (26-30). With her own experience of life as a married woman, she emphasises the ignorance of the young unmarried Chorus (142-50). She later thinks that things are turning out well, because she has learned that Heracles is returning safely, but she is wrong due to her initial ignorance of the identity of Iole. She also thinks that the anointed robe has a reasonable chance of winning Heracles back, but this proves false. Hyllus misunderstands his mother's intentions in sending the robe. Heracles in turn misunderstands the same matter, but is much less concerned about issues of intention. Instead, his own focus is upon his failure to have understood the oracles he received.

The failure of human knowledge is also presented in the play at times by having dramatic silence defeat speech.[11] Speech is often a vehicle for knowledge, as Deianeira's opening mention of an 'account known to mankind' suggests. On the other hand, silence emphasises the physical deed, in what is at times a kind of mute acceptance of reality. For example, when Deianeira and the Chorus first hear of Heracles' imminent arrival, Deianeira offers thanks and the Chorus sing an emotional song of happiness at the news. Yet these happy outbursts are silenced by the entry of the captives of Oichalia. These silent, wretched figures mark the reality of physical suffering, as opposed to Deianeira and the Chorus' (empty) expectations of a happy homecoming for Heracles. For it is the silent suffering of the captives, as opposed to the Chorus' song of happiness, that is ultimately the proper response, in the sense that it foreshadows the direction of the play, since the captives include, in the figure of the silent Iole, the catalyst that will lead to the tragic resolution of the drama. Similarly, Deianeira's silent exit to her suicide, in the face of the mistaken accusations of her son, again shows the reality of events overmastering human attempts to understand and assess them. Her silent exit marks the reality of her resolution to kill herself, a movement where final self-justifications are meaningless compared to the reality of her own death. Moreover, her silence marks the fact that *any* self-justification would be useless in the face of the fact that despite her best intentions she has killed her husband, that 'best of men'. In this regard husband and wife are united in their aristocratic outlook. For both Heracles and Deianeira, unlike Hyllus ('This is the whole of the matter: she erred while intending good', 1136), do not count her mistaken intention as a mitigating factor in assessing her action: mistaken or not, Deianeira has killed Heracles, and it is this which defines her character. Just as Deianeira offers no excuses, so Heracles accepts none. There is only the raw fact of murder.

This interpretation tries to show how the play gives a standard piece of popular wisdom greater specificity and force by arguing that the events of the play do not simply suggest the idea that late learning can have tragic results, but more disturbingly the idea that thought, reflection and words are simply inadequate to the violent reality of the world. Such a view gives a good account of the play's presentation of the theme of late learning, as initiated by Deianeira's opening words. For her use and interpretation of the idea that one should not measure one's life before death is fundamentally right: hers is an unhappy life. The saying and Deianeira's personal interpretation of it are in this sense correct. Yet on another level, they are both inadequate, in that this knowledge does not enable one to encompass the physical event, the reality of suffering. Deianeira is in the end reduced to silence in her misfortune, a silence that says more than her earlier attempts to describe or foresee her life. Thus the play does not simply assume a piece of traditional wisdom as valid, but demonstrates its truth in the most forceful way – by showing how it is ultimately useless. The truth of the maxim that one should not trust in premature, and so inadequate, judgements about one's life is proven, ironically, by the fact that Deianeira's own use of the maxim itself is premature and inadequate.

Yet if the beginning of the play is useful in drawing out the implications of the theme of late learning, the end of the play, with its final statement that 'none of this is not Zeus' (1278), reminds us that the gods do have the ability to know the future, and that this heavenly realm has had a large role to play in the story. Although no character understands the oracle before the event, the relation between human agent and oracle is different in the cases of Deianeira and Heracles. As has recently been emphasised, the oracles are not about Deianeira: rather, she is part of the means by which the oracles concerning Heracles, and gathered by Heracles, are ultimately shown to be true.[12] The fact that these oracles are not about her, and yet deeply affect her, is only one more example of Deianeira's dependence upon her husband for her own status and identity, as well as of the fundamental difference between the characters. For Deianeira the oracles are yet more evidence that she is unable to foresee, predict or encompass the future. Her possession of the oracles left by Heracles helps her no more than her reflective, generalising outlook. However, Heracles' relationship to the oracles, by the end of the play, is quite different from his wife's.

Unlike Deianeira, Heracles has an intimate connection with the oracles of the play. Not only are they about him, but they are derived ultimately from his own father, Zeus (1159-78), and hence both their relevance and authority are beyond question, even if their exact meaning is unclear. The fact that Heracles is a son of Zeus is emphasised throughout the play, and this only serves to mark that conditions for Heracles, as the son of the king of the gods, are not the same as those for other mortals. Yet, given his present plight, an ironic comment such as the Chorus' 'Who has seen Zeus so unconcerned for his children?' (139-40) suggests that being the son of Zeus does not mean an easier lot in life. Rather, it is because of Heracles' relationship to his father that he suffers as he does, since as a bastard son his labours are the result of his step-mother Hera's jealousy.

Yet if Heracles' relation to his father does not mean a happier life (if anything, the opposite), he does at the end of the play seem to benefit from his closer relationship to the gods. When he first awakes he is unable to master his suffering, crying out in lamentation, seeing himself as a passive victim of violence and pain. Yet when he hears from Hyllus that it was Nessus who provided the poison (1141-2), understanding breaks in upon him and his demeanour changes.[13] No longer does he simply focus on and display his sufferings, but instead he tells of his new-found understanding, and then, accepting his end, prepares for the future. He explains that both the oracle's statements have been proven accurate, that the dead (i.e. Nessus) have killed him, and that it is true that he is now obtaining respite from his labours. He then calls upon Hyllus to be obedient to him in his final requests. The timing here is important: just as Heracles has learned the truth of his father's oracles about him, and accepts them as his lot, so he in turn asks his own son to be obedient to him.[14] His demand of Hyllus that he bring him to Mount Oeta and commit him to the flames is a very physical, concrete manifestation of Heracles' acceptance of what has happened to him. In a sense, his new-found awareness that things have turned out in agreement with the oracles from his father leads him to master his physical suffering by performing an even more extreme act of violence. The robe is currently burning and melting away Heracles' body, but he will take this process in hand, by commanding Hyllus to commit him to a cleansing fire that will release him from both life and the agonies of the robe. Thus the 'cleanser' of Greece (1012) ultimately cleanses himself. Further, this act of self-command through violence returns Heracles to himself, in that we again have him acting in a fashion typical to him: combating the violent and monstrous with his own violence.

And yet the contrasts and ironies remain. Charles Segal emphasises that the man of action here at the end of the play displays a mental strength in his ability to commit himself to the flames, a mental strength that seems to result directly from his new understanding of the events that have befallen him as in accord with what was prophesied.[15] Hence his physical mastery is reasserted in a *passive* form, as endurance. Heracles no longer acts, but is acted upon, and his heroism consists in his ability to endure this suffering.[16] Hence the oracles ultimately produce in Heracles a result quite different from that which Deianeira experiences. Deianeira tried to encompass the brute reality of the world, whether in the form of her own suffering, or the force and inevitability of desire, by a sort of reductive reasoning ('I already know my life is wretched', 'desire is absolute'), and yet was unable to predict or deal with either the past or the future. In contrast, Heracles ultimately uses his knowledge to encompass and accept the physical reality of the world (although he too 'learns too late') just when it is finally threatening to overwhelm him. Thus we have a reversal similar to the one concerning the family; in a play which centred upon the breakdown of the family, the end result was the refashioning of the *oikos*. So here, in a play that continually emphasises the failure of human understanding to either foresee or deal with the reality of events, the result is a last reversal where knowledge, even if it is only the understanding that Heracles was meant to die at this time, is used to cope with present reality.

Yet while the human Deianeira and the soon-to-be-divine Heracles exist to some extent on different planes, and so are able to make use of the prophecies to very different degrees, ultimately the two are linked by the way that they both leave the stage in silence to go to their deaths. In both cases, the audience is still left with the raw physicality that characterises the play as a whole, its emphasis on the concrete deed over humankind's ephemeral, fallible, understanding, on objective (brute/animal) reality over the failed human comprehension of it.[17] For if Heracles, unlike Deianeira, ultimately does learn something from the oracles, it is a knowledge without positive content. He shows no foreknowledge whatsoever of his later deification.[18] Nor, as we noted, does he now act from any change in motives derived from a privileged source of knowledge, but he is still driven by the same relentless desire that has characterised him throughout. Thus Heracles shares in the play's overall emphasis on the futility of thought and language. These are his final words (1259-63):

> Come my unyielding soul, before rousing
> this disease again, suppress your cries,
> applying the stone-studded bit of steel,
> in order to accomplish as a source of gladness
> an unwished for deed.

Note that while earlier Heracles was feminised by his crying and general lack of verbal control, now his endurance is measured by his ability to be silent. Thus, even in his grim ending, Heracles reclaims a heroic finish to his (mortal) life by his silent endurance of the unavoidable force of the real: his acceptance suggests that he, unlike the others, has at least learned something from the tragedy of his house, even if this learning is only the 'idea' of heroic endurance itself. And while the audience may assume that Heracles is to be deified after his death, Heracles himself has no expectation that anything other than death is awaiting him.[19]

Hyllus reiterates with greater bitterness the theme of human ignorance, and with a greater emphasis on human suffering and the gods' apparent indifference to it (1270-4):

> Nobody foresees the future,
> but what has happened now is pitiable for us,
> and a source of shame to them [the gods],
> and harshest of all for the man
> enduring this suffering.

Hyllus refers not only to Heracles but also to the suffering of the family as a whole, including Hyllus himself. Hyllus has been forced to accept the will of his father, just as Heracles has been forced to accept the will of Zeus. Hyllus gets no explanation from Heracles, just as Heracles has no assurances from his father. Yet it is precisely this acceptance by Heracles that separates him from his son, who accuses where Heracles accedes. Thus by the end of the play the piece of conventional Greek wisdom that you cannot know the nature of your life until it is over is given back its paradoxical force; the statement ultimately imparts a knowledge of humankind's fundamental *lack* of knowledge, a knowledge with no positive content, a knowledge only of acceptance and endurance. The brutal and contradictory logic of the play is that ultimately even pessimism is insufficient as a response to the ignorance and suffering that affects human life. Thus if Athenian tragedy is 'the epistemological genre par excellence',[20] the *Women of Trachis* may be its most negative example.

## Gods and oracles

The fates of the human characters are directly related to the gods, and in particular to the will of Zeus. Zeus, as the greatest of the gods, was understood to rule and structure the universe so as to make of it an ordered whole, a cosmos, and thus in Greek thought it is common to attribute events to him.[21] Zeus' prominent role in the play[22] is emphasised early on when Deianeira in the prologue laments her life and the vicissitudes she has suffered, since she specifically relates her unstable fortune to him. She questions whether 'Zeus of contests' in fact concluded the battle between Heracles and Achelous in a beneficial manner for her, given her constant fears for the ever-absent hero (26-9, quoted above, pp. 42-3). So too by the end of the play Hyllus' (or the Chorus') final comment that 'None of these things is not Zeus' (1278) is emphatic in attributing the sorrows that have befallen the family to Zeus himself.

Traditional Greek religious thought assumed that mortal affairs were caused both by human agents and by the gods (a view often referred to as double determination). In *Iliad* Book

16, the Trojan hero Hector kills the Greek hero Patroclus and thereby wins great fame for himself, but he does so only with the help of the god Apollo. Thus this victory can be attributed to both Apollo and to Hector. But in the *Women of Trachis* the situation is in some ways rather one of *over*-determination. Not only is the play's action motivated and caused by both mortal and divine forces, but the tragedy that befalls Heracles' family is attributed to a plurality of agents and forces. As we have seen, Deianeira, Nessus and Heracles all play a crucial role in causing the events of the play. Even Iole can be understood as a cause of Heracles' death, since the desire she aroused in him led to Deianeira's use of the centaur's blood. It may be unfair to consider Iole, herself a victim of violence, as a cause of the play's misfortunes, but Hyllus in fact calls her at one point the 'sole partner' of his mother's death and of Heracles' sufferings (1233-4). Furthermore, on the divine level the source of causation is again not singular, since we have seen that both Zeus and Aphrodite (as the power of desire; see p. 79 above) are repeatedly presented as the cause behind the play's events.

However, within this profusion of agents, Zeus' role remains distinct. For unlike Aphrodite, who represents a particular causal force that resides within human beings (the force of desire), Zeus is the cause of the play's action in the wider sense that he regulates the cosmos as a whole.[23] The *parodos* of the Chorus (94-140) gives us some indication of the nature of his rule. The Chorus in this song criticise Deianeira for her pessimistic attitude, saying that Zeus has not ordained that humankind should only experience sorrow or only happiness. Rather, 'pain and grace/ circle around upon all,/ like the whirling paths of the Great Bear' (129-31). Zeus' rule, and in particular his treatment of humankind, is here compared to a constellation which was known in antiquity for its consistency of movement, thereby presenting an image of mutability within order.[24] Moreover, given that this order involves some sort of alternation of advantage and harm, the suggestion is that Zeus' order is itself founded upon a principle of balance, and is therefore just in nature.

However, the Chorus' comparison of Zeus' rule to the regular movement of the stars also has negative connotations for humankind. The Chorus cannot be claiming that good and harm comes to each individual *equally*, but only that every individual will experience both at some point in their life. It of course remains possible for a person to receive a predominantly good, or a predominantly bad, fortune. The play's presentation of Deianeira's life as one of persistent misfortune bitterly leavened by that one illusionary moment when she thinks Heracles is returning home safely to her (200-4), can be taken as a good example of this sort of imbalance.

Furthermore, like the gods themselves, the stars, being for the Greeks 'deathless', are distant entities which exist beyond the limits of mortal time. The pattern established by Zeus, in which good and evil is distributed in some regulated fashion, again need not mean equal portions of good and evil given to each individual, but rather some sort of overall balance of good and harm to humans generally or universally. That is, harm for one individual could be understood to be balanced by good for another. This conception of cosmic justice, one which extends beyond individuals and even generations, is most often associated with the tragedian Aeschylus and his trilogy the *Oresteia*, but it has been argued that such a view of the gods' justice is also to be found in Sophocles.[25] Heracles himself can be understood as a good example of someone who experiences this sort of imbalance. His was the paradigmatic life of toil, and specifically toil in the service of others, as he says himself (1010-13, quoted p. 60 above).

This suggestion concerning the nature of Zeus' rule can be strengthened if we consider how the characters are often presented as suffering as a result of other peoples' actions, rather than simply as a result of their own. We have already suggested that the sufferings of the family of Heracles, resulting from a rift between husband and wife, can be understood to respond to the rift between husband and wife on the divine level, since all of Heracles' suffering ultimately can be traced back to Hera's anger at Zeus' act of infidelity which produced Heracles himself. Similarly, although Deianeira certainly shares responsibility for the catastrophe that over-takes her family and herself (see pp. 52-60 above), she is also, in terms of the will of the gods, simply a means to an end. The second oracle emphasises the role of Nessus as the one in Hades (i.e. someone dead) who will nonetheless kill Heracles. That Heracles should die in recompense for the deaths of all those monsters he himself killed suggests a certain balance and order in the workings of the cosmos, but one which is also cruel in its scale and method, since Deianeira's death is only a means to effect this balance. Importantly, there seems to be little or no individual moral aspect to this balance. The play does not concern itself with the issue of whether it was right or not for Heracles to kill Nessus, and hence whether it is right that Heracles should in turn be killed by Nessus. One death simply balances the other.[26]

This sort of universal order, one which shows little concern for the individual even as it creates a total, general balance among the parts, is particularly well seen if we consider the workings of desire within the play. It was seen that desire was presented as a universal force, that all were subject to its power. Moreover, it typically affects people as both a positive and as a negative force. Heracles' desire for Deianeira made her the wife of 'the best of men', just as her own desire leads to long nights of anxiety for him in his absence. Yet it is desire's regulated and impersonal movement between individuals that best captures the sense of an order that operates without regard for these individuals. Deianeira sees in Iole the image of herself at a younger age, as a woman whose beauty ultimately brings her sorrow. Moreover, in her reflective manner, Deianeira is fully aware of how desire functions (547-9):

> I see the youth of one proceeding as the other recedes.
> A man's eye loves to pluck the bloom
> of the former, but it avoids the latter

Human desire for the beautiful can only emphasise the fleeting nature of human beauty itself, and there is a simple structure at work in Heracles' transfer of desire from the older Deianeira to the younger Iole, as Deianeira herself acknowledges. Since it was her own desire-causing beauty that won her Heracles, she now feels compelled to accept that Heracles' desire has shifted to Iole.

In one regard the Chorus' comparison of Zeus' order to the movements of the constellation of the Great Bear in the *parodos* is quite misleading. Since the constellation was known for its *regulated* movement, the Chorus' words suggest that Zeus' distribution of advantage and harm is something that can be transparently known by humankind itself. Yet as we saw in our discussion of the theme of the limits of human knowledge, the figures of the play are typically characterised by their *inability* to understand the workings of divine will.

This gap between Zeus' cosmic order and human comprehension of it is dramatised by the play's use of oracles.[27] Deianeira states early in the play that Heracles left an oracle written on a tablet which stated, in Deianeira's words (79-81):

That either he is going to come to the end of his life,
or, upon completing this labour, he is going
to have a happy life in the future.

The ambiguity here is that the two choices in fact refer to the same outcome, as Heracles makes clear when he speaks of the oracle (1169-73)

Which said that in the present and living moment
an end would be made of the toils set upon me.
I figured I was going to fare well,
But it was nothing other than my own death.
For the dead do not toil.

Thus we only learn by the end of the play that the two options expressed in Deianeira's version of the oracle only reflect the oracle and Heracles' *mistaken interpretation* of it. There was never any option, only a single prediction misunderstood in a positive manner. The resolution of this oracle must suggest a certain amount of pessimism about human action and human will, since what was presented as a choice ends as a simple prediction of death. Moreover Heracles' inability to comprehend the oracle is all the more emphatic for the fact that it is derived from the Selloi, priests of the oracle of his own father at Dodona (1166-7).

The case is the same with the oracle involving Nessus' posthumous revenge, as Heracles' comments show (1159-63):

> For long ago Zeus prophesied to me
> that I would die by no one who lived,
> but by one who was dead and dwelled in Hades.
> And so this beast the centaur, as the divinity
> prophesised, has killed me, he dead and me alive.

This second oracle once again reveals the same human inability to understand the divine order. The unexpressed but obvious point is that Heracles did not fear the oracle because it seemingly forecast the impossible, but Nessus' posthumous revenge ultimately proves the oracle correct. And given that the two oracles in effect duplicate each other in their basic function of predicting Heracles' death, they can only increase the sense of inevitability that surrounds Heracles' downfall. Just as the play presents a plurality of agents to whom Heracles' death can be attributed (Nessus, Deianeira, Iole, Aphrodite, Zeus), so too do the two oracles produce a sense of over-determination in the matter of Heracles' fate.

If this suggests a certain sense of fatalism in the play's presentation of the relationship between gods and humans, a few counterbalancing points should be made. First, oracles do not cause the events they describe, but simply predict them. Heracles does not die because the oracles said he would: he dies because of the network of causal factors that the play dramatises. Secondly, if Zeus regulates and orders the cosmos, including human life, he does not do so in an interventionist manner. The specific causal forces that produce the events of the drama are altogether mortal in nature: Heracles' desire, Deianeira' jealousy, Nessus' wish for revenge. Thus the order that Zeus establishes for mortal kind is not produced by compelling human action from without, but rather it operates through the nature of humankind itself. As a result, questions of free-will and determinism are largely irrelevant here. We might say that the human characters of the play must act as they do, and that they yet act in accordance with their own desires and wishes. The free play of human nature is itself one part of the overall structure by which Zeus rules the universe. And if the mortal characters are in some sense 'fated' to fall, it remains true that the fates which afflict them are still meaningfully understood to be *their* fates.

### The apotheosis of Heracles

One question that scholars have continually addressed is whether the play makes allusion to the apotheosis of Heracles. The question is a central one, since allusion to such a later deification would mitigate the otherwise highly negative ending of the play.

By the time of the original fifth-century BC production of the *Women of Trachis* the Greeks generally recognised and worshipped Heracles as either a hero or a god, or as both, whereas in earlier times they tended to view him strictly as a mortal hero who upon his death went to Hades as a shade.[28] Moreover, the story of Heracles' death on the pyre on Mount Oeta was already well known, although it is less clear whether the apotheosis of Heracles was specifically linked with his death on the pyre. Our play makes a number of references to Mount Oeta (e.g. 1191, 436-7), and these may hint at a later event in the myth which happened after Heracles' death, i.e. his apotheosis from the pyre on Mount Oeta. On a more general level of allusion, the play's constant reference to Heracles as Zeus' son might also be a means of raising in the minds of the audience the question of the apotheosis of Heracles. Whether or not these aspects of the text allude to the apotheosis, there is certainly nothing to *prevent* an audience member from recalling or reflecting upon those versions of the myth that did present Heracles as obtaining a blessed life among the gods after his death. We have seen in the case of Deianeira (in particular in the matter of her motivation) that the play does indeed manipulate audience response by playing against different versions of the myth. Presumably the audience's awareness of mythic variants cannot simply be turned on at one point and turned off at another, but rather was constantly present in shaping the response of the historical audience.

On the other hand, it remains true that the play does not explicitly refer to the apotheosis, let alone dramatising the event. Further, Heracles and the other characters show no awareness of such an eventuality, and we have seen that the final words of the play are pessimistic in nature. Some have felt that if the play is understood as alluding to the later apotheosis of Heracles then the emphasis on Heracles' ability to master his suffering becomes largely meaningless, since such human endurance would signify little in the light of the fact that Heracles will shortly enjoy the blessed and painless life of a god.[29]

A recent study by Margalit Finkelberg is helpful here. First, Finkelberg argues for a textual emendation for the final, corrupt line of the second *stasimon* (662) that would make it refer to a religious rite dealing with Heracles' apotheosis from the pyre which was performed upon Mount Oeta in historical times, thus producing a direct reference to Heracles' later existence as a god.[30] This point must remain speculative given that it depends on a textual correction. However, Finkelberg, following the persuasive account of Holt for the acceptance of an allusion to the apotheosis at the end of the play,[31] also argues that we should see dramatic irony in this reference to the later apotheosis. That is, although the characters do not recognise that Heracles, by committing himself to the flames, will be transformed into a god, the historical audience would have done so. Moreover, this reference would mean that the oracle which stated that Heracles would die or accomplish an end to his labours should not be understood as presenting a choice between death or death (as Heracles understands it), but death or immortality.[32]

I agree with Finkelberg view that the audience's awareness of the deification of Heracles on Mount Oeta should be included in our assessment of the play's final impact. What is refreshing about her argument is that, unlike some other scholars, she does not assume that a clear-cut allusion to the apotheosis must diminish the force or effect of the play.[33] Rather, by her view, the final effect of the play will simply be a different one: tragic in so far as we have seen the human characters, including Heracles, suffer before our eyes, but positive and uplifting in so far as we know that Heracles will be rewarded with immortality for his labours. Following Hugh Lloyd-Jones, she suggests that the play thus allows the audience to see beyond human limitations into the plans of Zeus.[34]

Viewing the ending of the play in a more positive light allows us to see the work in new and interesting ways. Where we might part company with Finkelberg is in her view that such an allusion at the end of the play must produce a *singular* response. Finkelberg, following Stinton, argues that 'either the belief in the apotheosis is absent from the *Trachiniae*, and then we have one tragedy, or it is found there, and then we have another, entirely different, one'.[35] That such a belief will create a different tragedy is certainly true. However, Finkelberg seems to see the meaning of the play as fully inherent *in* the play: it is either 'there', or it is 'not there'. Yet an allusion, like language in general, creates meaning through the interaction between word and recipient. And different recipients, even if from the same community of a given historical moment, can and will generate different meanings. Both of the two different tragedies that Finkelberg discusses may be present simultaneously.

For instance, even if every single member of the audience responded to the play with an awareness of the contemporary rituals and myths that presented Heracles as a god, this does not guarantee that everyone must have *believed* that Heracles was in fact deified. No doubt most did, but the fifth century was a time when traditional religious beliefs were being questioned. We have criticisms of traditional religion as early as Xenophanes (*c.* 570 – *c.* 475 BC), and in the case of Heracles himself, a passage in Herodotus specifically presents different views about whether Heracles was a god, hero or man.[36] The issue is too large to go into in detail here, but there is undoubtedly sufficient evidence to show that we cannot simply assume that the historical audience all responded the same way, that they all understood the play in the ironic fashion argued for by Finkelberg because they simply 'knew' that Heracles was deified. This is to make the mistake that was discussed in Chapter 2, i.e. to believe that knowledge of 'the' historical audience will give us a singular understanding of the play. Many may indeed have responded in the way that Finkelberg suggests, but others may have continued to wonder why the play neither depicts the apotheosis nor refers to it in an explicit fashion.

Such a lack of certainty on the part of the audience is all the more likely when we consider two further points. First, dramatic irony may function differently at the end of the play. Finkelberg compares the *Women of Trachis'* ironic ending to the way Sophocles often presents a joyous choral song that is afterwards undercut by a negative turn of events.[37] For example, the joyous choral song at *Women of Trachis* 205-24 in response to the imminent return of Heracles is overturned by the later realisation that he has first sent home Iole as Deianeira's replacement. Yet in cases like these, the irony is confirmed in the course of the play: that is, if the Chorus' song is ironic for the audience, in that the audience suspects that Heracles will not arrive home happily, it is only when Heracles does arrive on the verge of death, and suffer a tragic fall, that the audience's superior knowledge is confirmed.[38] But at the end of a play, there is nothing further to confirm or undermine such knowledge: it is, contra Finkelberg, not 'there', but in the minds of the audience members, and so depends upon them for its presence and effect. This uncertainty is enhanced by the *Women of Trachis'* intense focus upon the limitations of human knowledge. Indeed, if we recall the play's opening maxim as formulated by Deianeira, that you should not count yourself fortunate, or not until you reach the end of your life, we can see a different sort of irony in the play's ending. For by not actually presenting or explicitly referring to the apotheosis, the play does not present us with 'the end' that would allow us to make a final assessment of the life of Heracles. The play leaves the audience to supply such sure knowledge from their own contemporary experience of Heracles as god and hero, while at the same time suggesting that this knowledge may not in fact be so sure.[39] Here is the Nurse's reformulation of the maxim after she has seen Deianeira kill herself (943-6):

> So that anyone who
> reckons two or even more days ahead
> is foolish: for there is in fact no tomorrow
> before one has fared well today.

Heracles' exit to Mount Oeta can be seen as further proof of this maxim, and also as an ironic comment upon it, for unlike Deianeira, who is dead when the Nurse speaks, he has not yet reached his end. The general point is well made by Deborah Roberts:

> we are made to understand – if we pay attention to these allu-sions – that our judgement at the end of the play (which may itself be a complex judgement), though grounded in the play's action, is inevitably provisional, and that *we will not be able to remedy that provisional nature*. (italics added)[40]

Debate over this aspect of the play will no doubt continue. However, Finkelberg's reading provides a suitable conclusion as it allows us to reiterate that works of art do not interpret them-selves. The historical contexts of the original audience, some of which have been examined in this study, helped shape their response to the play. Yet we should note that a clear conse-quence of this position is that our own contexts will also help to produce what the work means for us. Self-awareness of *our* contribution to the production of the work's meaning is there-fore the logical and necessary counterpart to such historical reconstruction. For the force of the present can no more be ignored than that of the past. However, our present-day conditions are not something that need to be 'added' to our interpretations: they are already present in those interpretations, helping to determine and define them. Not only do present-day concerns help determine the types of questions we address to the play, they also help determine just how the text is able to answer these questions. For example, the emphasis on character in our study reflects the modern-day emphasis on the individual, but also requires us to try to rethink our own assumptions about character if we are to see how the play may have affected its original audience. But although such concerns do help to determine our questions and answers, they do not do so entirely. The play is a historical object that reaches us by means of a literary tradition, an accumulation of historical contexts and receptions that provide their own force and impetus. Thus we do not simply interpret the play as we wish any more than we recreate the past: rather there is a fusion of past and present.[41] As a result, interpretation can be understood as a product of both history and our own particular reception of this history. The belief in complete interpretative freedom, the idea that we can understand the text any way we like, is therefore as much a myth as the traditional view that there is a single, stable, and therefore definitive meaning for any given work of art.

Finally, it should be understood that to recognise our own contributions to the work's meaning does not mean that we are producing purely subjective interpretations. Rather, we are producing interpretations that answer to certain sets of historical factors. This is how the *Women of Trachis* itself functioned when originally experienced by its fifth-century Athenian audience. Part of the project of understanding an artistic work is to come to recognise just how these historical factors shape our responses. Moreover, because we are interested in this original set of circumstances, because one of our present-day concerns is precisely an interest in history, our interpretations can overlap with theirs, even as we make the play our own.

# 7

# Reception

As we have seen, a work can be studied in terms of its immediate historical conditions (a synchronic approach). But it can also be studied in terms of the reception of the work through time (a diachronic approach). 'Reception theory' examines the combination of the two approaches.[1] What such studies primarily show us is how the work, with its accumulation of historical interpretations, has come down to us with certain values and meanings attached to it.[2] Yet this approach also leads us to recognise that a work's meaning and effect are dependent upon historical conditions that are always subject to change.

The reception of the mythical figure of Heracles has been incredibly rich: even in ancient Greece the character that began no doubt as a folk-hero strongman[3] became a god and a hero throughout Greece, an ethical paradigm for Greek intellectuals,[4] and a source of fun in his comic personifications.[5] He was a figure who over time was adapted to multiple roles, from a panhellenic hero of Greek political unity in the fourth century BC (Isocrates' *Oration to Philip*) to a virtuous medieval knight in the fifteenth century AD (Raoul Le Fèvre's *Recueil des hystoires de Troyes*).

In looking at the history of Sophocles' *Women of Trachis*, three points are particularly important. First, as we have seen, the *Women of Trachis* is itself already a 'reception', a reworking, based upon fifth-century concerns and interests, of older stories (see pp. 30-5 above). Secondly, one of the few concrete facts we do know about the play's ancient reception is that it was chosen as part of a collection of seven dramas by Sophocles and widely circulated as a text for teaching. This may indicate that the *Women of Trachis* was viewed as one of Sophocles' 'best', or perhaps simply most representative, works. Whether or not we would agree with this view, the canonisation of the play meant that this particular version was destined to exert a greater influence upon the tradition than other versions. However, the third point is that the *Women of Trachis* has not had anywhere near the popularity, as measured by either re-performance or adaptation, of the other extant works of Sophocles.[6] This may be because in many ways the *Women of Trachis* does not agree with traditional perceptions of Sophocles, and is often viewed as less mature or less realised than his other surviving works. The play does, however, have an interesting (if small) reception, and I conclude by examining some of the more important adaptations of the story that are more directly dependent upon Sophocles' *Women of Trachis*: Ovid's *Heroides* IX, the *Hercules Oetaeus*,[7] attributed to Seneca but probably by an imitator, the free translation by the modernist poet Ezra Pound, first published in 1953 and performed on BBC radio in 1954, and Hansgünther Heyme's production of the play in Köln, Germany in 1976.

In *Heroides* IX, the Roman poet Ovid's account of the story of Deianeira and Heracles is presented in the form of a letter from Deianeira to Heracles in which she complains of the introduction of Iole into her home. This letter ends with Deianeira learning of the disastrous effects of the robe, and with her decision to commit suicide. While it is clear that Ovid has used a number of different sources, it is equally clear that his central source was Sophocles' *Women of Trachis*, a debt that can be seen both on the level of a similarity in plotting, and in numerous points of theme and vocabulary.[8] Yet what is most interesting about these correspondences is that they often serve to show how Ovid himself understood Sophocles' play, as frequently *Heroides* IX reads as a commentary and interpretation of the *Women of Trachis*. For example, Ovid's Deianeira states explicitly the condition that afflicts both her and Sophocles' Deianeira (27-32):

Just as ill-matched cattle at the plough proceed badly,
so afflicted is the wife who is less than her great husband.
For those bearing the burden it is not a source of honour, but a
    pretence that harms;
If you wish to marry well, marry your equal.

We saw above some of the ways this distance between Heracles
and Deianeira was dramatised in the *Women of Trachis*, and the
passage quoted from *Heroides* IX reads as an implicit commentary on Sophocles: Ovid's Deianeira, whom Ovid's readers
probably would have compared with her famous predecessor in
the *Women of Trachis*, is thereby presented as that much more
aware of her predicament.

Also of interest is Ovid's treatment of the figure of Iole and
her entry into the house of Deianeira and Heracles. Like the
Iole of the *Women of Trachis*, Ovid's Iole stands out by virtue of
her dress, but unlike in Sophocles' play, she also stands out by
her triumphant attitude:

She does not come in the manner of a captive, with dishevelled
    hair,
with a proper visage showing her lot;
She comes, apart, resplendent in much gold,
just as you yourself were dressed in Phrygia.[9]
She looks loftily upon the crowd, as if Hercules had been defeated;
You would think Oechalia stood, and that her father lived.

Here again Ovid interprets his literary predecessor. For we saw
that while Iole in the *Women of Trachis* was presented as
sorrowful at what had befallen her and her family (322-8),
Deianeira herself assumed that Iole was in love with Heracles
(443-4) and that she would gain some sort of fame from her
relationship with Heracles (550-1). Hence Deianeira of the
*Women of Trachis* seems to envision Iole as a potential rival in
desire for Heracles, rather than simply as a victim of Heracles'
own uncontrolled lust. And it is this attitude that Ovid explicitly attributes to his Iole, since she is presented by Deianeira in
*Heroides* IX as a confident victor. To put it briefly, if anachronistically, Ovid rewrites the *Women of Trachis* by transferring

Deianeira's latent fears of Iole onto the character of Iole herself. Further, this adaptation is an example of the dominant theme of *Heroides* IX, the shameful subjugation of Heracles by women, which is itself a more explicit presentation of a theme found in Sophocles' original.[10]

The *Hercules Oetaeus* also depends in good part upon the *Women of Trachis* of Sophocles, as can be seen from any number of similarities in scenes and language. Moreover, as with Ovid, the later writer's work tends to explain or answer the earlier. Thus while Sophocles' Heracles longs to kill Deianeira with his own hands although she has already committed suicide (e.g. 1064-9), Deianeira in the *Hercules Oetaeus* hesitates at one point to kill herself specifically in order to *allow* Hercules to kill her (970-82; note the repeated reference to 'hands' in both plays). Yet the differences are equally important. In particular, the *Hercules Oetaeus* can be understood as being adapted to present the story in light of Stoic beliefs.[11] Among other aspects of this philosophical school, such as a heavy emphasis on duty, the Stoics valued endurance and fortitude, especially in the matter of one's death. As Seneca himself wrote, 'it takes a whole life to learn how to die' (*On the Brevity of Life* 7.4).[12] The *Hercules Oetaeus* tends to emphasise those elements of the Sophoclean account that fit well with this Stoic outlook. Thus it focuses especially upon Heracles' heroic death, greatly expanding on the *Women of Trachis'* treatment of the same subject (see 1259-63). Comments in the *Hercules Oetaeus* such as those found at 1481-2 ('Now let me choose a death fully worthy of me, resplendent, renowned and famed') and at 1675 ('How peacefully he bore what was given to him!') emphasise this Stoic outlook. Similarly, in the *Hercules Oetaeus* there are repeated and lengthy references throughout the play to the labours of Hercules in such a way as to focus on his endurance, duty and contribution to humankind's well-being (e.g. 1188-1206, 1235-64), whereas in Sophocles' play, as we have seen, Heracles' role as a civilising force for humankind is presented in a more ambivalent manner, undermined as it is by his role as a force destructive of civilisation. The *Hercules*

*Oetaeus* also contains a major change in its handling of the character of Deianeira. Restraint of one's emotions was another central tenet of Stoic philosophy. Whereas Deianeira in the *Women of Trachis* continually tries to restrain the emotional effects of *erôs* upon herself, Deianeira is presented in the *Hercules Oetaeus* as an example of an individual who is uncontrolled in her passions, serving as a negative foil to Heracles who in his death ultimately masters fear and pain.

What confronts the reader of Pound's version of the *Women of Trachis* are his efforts to make the play work within a contemporary context. In order to have the past speak more clearly to the present (a central concern in his translations, just as translation itself was central to his poetry), Pound tends to translate the Greek into colloquial English. As an example I give a fairly literal translation of Hyllus' angry address to his mother, followed by Pound's translation of the same lines (734-7):

> Mother, how I would have chosen one of three things concerning
>     you;
> either that you were no longer living, or, if alive,
> called the mother of another, or that you exchanged
> a better mind than this, your present one.
>
> Damn you, I wish you were dead,
> or no mother, anyhow, or at any rate not mine.

Pound certainly takes liberties with the Greek, and scholars have often criticised his translations on such grounds.[13] However, Pound has made a thoughtful attempt to recreate the passage, if not faithfully to translate it. For instance, Hyllus' choice of three evils was a common rhetorical trope in ancient Greek.[14] To recreate this sense of the familiar in English, Pound has simply used the common curse 'damn you, I wish you were dead': in both cases, the familiarity of the language suggests the passion of the speaker. Moreover, the confused logic of 'no mother, anyhow, or at least not mine' also catches something of the agitation in the original. Finally, Pound has kept the three-part structure of the sentence ('dead ... no mother ... not mine') with the use of his own, much shorter, ascending tricolon, even though he has edited out the final part of Hyllus' original statement ('or that you had exchanged ...'). What Pound has translated from the original passage is a sense of emotional urgency conveyed by means of a distinctive yet direct form of language.

Consider also Pound's rendition of the final lines of the *Women of Trachis'* third *stasimon* (851-61):

> LET the tears flow.
>   Ne'er had bright Herakles in his shining
> Need of pity till now
>   whom fell disease burns out.
> How swift on Oechal's height
>   to take a bride.
> Black pointed shaft that shielded her in flight,
> Attest
> That
> Kupris stood by and never said a word,
> Who now flares here the contriver
> manifest ...
> and indifferent.
> [The dea ex machina, hidden behind a grey gauze in
> her niche, is lit up strongly so that the gauze is
> transparent. The apparition is fairly sudden, the
> fade-out slightly slower: the audience is almost in
> doubt that she has appeared.] (pp. 54-5)

Pound again does not translate the original Greek literally. For instance, his 'bright Herakles in his shining' derives more from his understanding of Herakles as 'the Solar vitality' (as he is described in the Personae, p. 24) than from the original Greek.[15] Yet his rendering of the final lines of the *stasimon* is powerful. In particular, while 'indifferent' goes beyond a literal translation, I suggest it shows both a sensitive reading of the Greek, and a sensitive reading of the play as a whole. The Greek word here is *amphipolos*, a common epithet of Aphrodite (or Kupris, an alternate name for the goddess), and it typically means 'attendant', presumably here in the sense that she 'attends' Heracles, since it was he who has been acting most conspicuously under her influence. Yet the word could also be literally translated as 'active on both sides', and I presume that this is where Pound's 'indifferent', in the sense of 'affecting all equally', is derived. And indeed, such a reading works well, for at this point of the play it is no revelation that *Heracles* has been acting under the spell of Aphrodite; rather the revelation is that Aphrodite has been behind the motives of *both* the principal characters. The reference here at the end of the song to the fact that Aphrodite has affected both Deianeira and Heracles 'indifferently' looks forward to the following description of Deianeira's death, which itself emphasises her own desire, since she stabs herself over her marriage bed. We have seen that it is quite apt to understand Aphrodite as a central operative force within the drama. Hence Pound's translation in this regard freely but meaningfully interprets a point of detail in the Greek that in turn helps to reinforce a central theme of the drama. Further, his introduction of the stage direction to reveal momentarily the goddess herself, while certainly not in the original production, is a forceful visual complement.

In his production of the play Heyme similarly chose to dramatise the play's depiction of sexual power in a concrete visual fashion.[16] The production began with the Chorus, removed from the acting area, mixing clay which they then used to fashion two straw puppets. At the end of the play, the Chorus entered the acting area and set up the two puppets, a female and a male, which were equipped with exaggerated sexual attributes. Such exaggeration can be taken to signify the central role of physical desire in the play. Moreover, given that these sexual attributes were presented on puppets, an obvious interpretation is that sexual desire can reduce the human individual to an automaton, a slave to her or his own desires. However, since the puppets were made of straw, the sexual attributes also had a flimsy aspect to them, and hence they could be understood to represent both sexual desire and human weakness. Thus this visual presentation nicely captured the play's depiction of the preponderance of desire in human life, even as it suggested how desire can weaken and destroy those it affects.

# Notes

Full details of all works cited in these notes by name and short title are given in the Bibliography below.

## Preface

**1**. The play's title is transliterated as *Trakhiniai* or *Trachiniai* (from the ancient Greek). *Trachiniae* is the Latin spelling of the title.

**2**. Aristotle *Poetics* 8, 1451a16-35.

**3**. As influentially described by Knox in *The Heroic Temper*.

**4**. Schlegel's assessment in the nineteenth century was particularly harsh: 'The *Trachiniae* appears to me to be so very inferior to the other pieces of Sophocles which have reached us, that I could wish there were some warrant for supposing that this tragedy was composed in the age, indeed, and in the school of Sophocles, perhaps by his son Iophon, and that it was by mistake attributed to the father. There is much both in the structure and plan, and in the style of the piece, calculated to excite suspicion'. (Quoted from Dawe, *Heritage*, pp. 169-70.)

**5**. For my own understanding and appreciation of the play, the studies of Easterling, Segal, Winnington-Ingram, Heiden, Seale, Ormand and Wohl have been particularly helpful.

## 1. Summary of the Play

**1**. This division derives from Aristotle *Poetics* 12, 1452b14-27, although in practice the surviving plays are often more fluid in structure.

**2**. The short choral song at 205-24 is generally not considered a formal *stasimon*.

**3**. Trachis is located near the eastern coast of Greece by the Malian gulf, just below Thessaly.

**4**. Euboea is the large island located north-east of Athens and Attica.

**5**. However, note that the play was probably not named as such by Sophocles, but by later editors of the play. Many plays are named after the Chorus even when it is not central to the action.

**6**. On the sustained use of dramatic irony in the choral songs in the *Women of Trachis* (ironic because they tend to express moods that the audience can recognise as being out of step with the coming events of the play), see Burton, *The Chorus in Sophocles' Tragedies*, p. 83.

**7**. Cenaeum is the north-west promontory of Euboea, just across from the Malian Gulf.

**8**. Note that while Lichas is being deceptive in his account (primarily by avoiding any mention of Iole), a number of elements of his story are familiar from other versions of the myth, and so are not simply lies, making the whole speech an intriguing mixture of falsehood and accuracy. See Scodel, *Sophocles*, pp. 34-5 for a good discussion of the speech.

**9**. See Easterling, *Commentary*, pp. 155-6 for discussion, and Finkelberg, 'Second Stasimon', pp. 130-9.

**10**. On this theme, see Easterling, 'Sophocles, *Trachiniae*', pp. 64-5, Segal, *Tragedy and Civilization*, pp. 65-73 and Segal, *Tragic World*, pp. 55-8.

**11**. This agrees with the tradition that is was either the hero Philoctetes, or his father Poias, who lit the pyre.

**12**. We are unsure who speaks the final four lines of the play, with a majority arguing that they are spoken by the Chorus, as typical of Athenian tragedy, with others assigning them to Hyllus.

## 2. Context

**1**. This modern notion that art should be autonomous from its social contexts is traced and described by Bourdieu, *The Rules of Art*.

**2**. See Barbara Goff in her (ed.), *History, Tragedy, Theory*, pp. 1-37 for a challenging but helpful look at the use of modern literary theory in Classics.

**3**. I use the term 'ideology' in a loose sense, meaning a collection of beliefs that shape, typically without being acknowledged, how individuals in a given society understand their world. For a good discussion, see Pelling, 'Tragedy and Ideology', pp. 224-35 in his (ed.), *Greek Tragedy and the Historian*.

**4**. The Delian league was a federation of city-states led by Athens. At first all members contributed ships to the league for the purpose of pursing the war against Persia in Asia Minor, but later tribute was given by the lesser city-states in lieu of ships. On the Delian League, see Fornara and Samons, *Athens from Cleisthenes to Pericles*, ch. 3.

**5**. On the reforms of Cleisthenes, see Manville, *The Origins of Citizenship in Ancient Athens*, pp. 185-209 and Ober, *Mass and Elite*, pp. 68-73.

**6**. For a history of this development, see Ober, *Mass and Elite*, pp. 53-103.

**7**. See Ober, *Mass and Elite*, pp. 289-92.

**8**. On the *oikos* in general see Pomeroy, *Families*, pp. 20-39. On heredity, the family and the individual, see Pomeroy, *Families*, ch. 2.

**9**. Jones, *On Aristotle and Greek Tragedy*, pp. 83-4, succinctly terms the *oikos* 'a psycho-physical community of the living and the dead and the unborn'.

**10**. The stability of such roles is a primary concern for Athenian tragedy, as is most famously seen in Sophocles' *Oedipus Rex*, where Oedipus' act of incest is referred to in terms that emphasise the fact that this transgression has led to the confusion and breakdown of family roles, with Oedipus as both son and husband to his mother and as father and sibling to his children (e.g. 1403-8, 1496-9).

**11**. On Athenian tragedy and Athenian citizenship generally, see Goldhill, *Reading Greek Tragedy*, pp. 58-69.

**12**. For a good up-to-date survey of our knowledge of fifth-century Athenian marriage, and its relationship to marriage in Athenian tragedy, see Foley, *Female Acts*, pp. 59-105.

**13**. See Gould, 'Law, Custom and Myth', pp. 49-50.

**14** On the legal status of women in Athens, see Gould, 'Law, Custom and Myth', pp. 3-46 and Foley, *Female Acts*, pp. 73-9.

**15**. This anxiety can be seen clearly e.g. in the first work of the corpus of the speechwriter Lysias (*c.* 459 – *c.* 388) in which a husband talks of how he kept a close eye on his new wife when she first moved into his home.

**16**. See Gould, 'Law, Custom and Myth', p. 53. For an idealised description of how a husband 'educates' his wife, see Xenophon *Oeconomicus* vii.4-x.13.

**17**. On the Panathenaic festival, see Burkert, *Greek Religion*, pp. 232-4.

**18**. The most famous example of weaving and its connection to the perceived deceptive nature of women is Penelope's deception of her suitors in the *Odyssey*, where she puts off their attempts to marry her by saying she will choose one of them only when she has finished weaving a shroud, a shroud which she secretly unweaves each night.

**19**. See Cairns, *Aidos*, pp. 228-41.

**20**. Compare Goldhill, p. 116 in Winkler and Zeitlin, *Nothing to Do with Dionysos*: 'the hero does not simply *reverse* the norms of what it means to fit into society but *makes a problem* of such integration'.

**21**. For the intersection of mythic past and contemporary Athens, see Vernant and Vidal-Naquet, *Tragedy and Myth*, pp. 9-14. Heiden, *Rhetoric*, p. 157, makes the suggestion that the *Women of Trachis*, in the way that it emphasises the spectator's or listener's role in the interpretation of myth, is thereby more democratic in its use of myth, since mythic narratives of various sorts were often used by aristocratic families to validate and legitimate their prominence in Greek society (typically as direct descendants of gods, and as those in charge of various cults).

**22**. On the categories of *philos* and *ekhthros* see Blundell, *Helping Friends and Harming Enemies*, ch. 2, Mitchell, *Greeks Bearing Gifts*, ch. 1, and Belfiore, 'Problematic Reciprocity in Greek Tragedy', pp. 139-58 in Gill et al. (eds), *Reciprocity in Ancient Greece*.

**23**. *Poetics* 14, 1453b19-22: 'When suffering exists among *philoi*, such as when a brother kills a brother (or is about to, or to do some such action), or a son his father, or a mother her son, or a son his mother – this is what is wanted.'

**24**. See Scodel, *Sophocles*, ch. 3 and Wohl, *Intimate Commerce*, part 1 for fuller examinations of the importance of exchange in the play.

**25**. Goldhill, pp. 127-9 in Winkler and Zeitlin, *Nothing to Do with Dionysos*, suggests that while tragedy is a suitable offering to the god Dionysus as the god of transgression, the plays themselves are the very opposite of ritual, since ritual attempts to keep things the same by a repetition of form, while the tragedies characteristically question what is considered normative.

**26**. On the Greater Dionysia, see Pickard-Cambridge, *Dramatic Festivals*, pp. 57-101, and Goldhill, pp. 97-129 in Winkler and Zeitlin, *Nothing to Do with Dionysos*.

**27**. Sophocles was frequently a winner of the top prize (18 times, compared to 13 for Aeschylus and 5 for Euripides).

**28**. See Hansen, *Democracy and Demography*.

**29**. See Goldhill, pp. 62-6 in Easterling, *Cambridge Companion*, for a recent discussion of the evidence.

**30**. See Csapo and Slater, *Context*, pp. 301-5, especially entries numbered 159, 166, and 167.

**31**. On the audience in general, see Pickard-Cambridge, *Dramatic Festivals*, pp. 263-78, Csapo and Slater, *Context*, pp. 286-305 and Goldhill, ch. 3 in Easterling, *Cambridge Companion*.

**32**. For a prejudiced picture of such a mob mentality at public events in Athens, see Plato *Republic* 492b-c.

**33**. See further Erp Taalman Kip, *Reader and Spectator*, ch. 5.

**34**. See Wilson, *The Athenian Institution of the Khoregia*.

**35**. For a good discussion of the Chorus in this regard, see Gould, 'Tragedy and Collective Experience', pp. 217-43 in Silk (ed.), *Tragedy and the Tragic*. On the Chorus in general see Pickard-Cambridge, *Dramatic Festivals*, pp. 232-62 and Csapo and Slater, *Context*, pp. 349-68.

**36**. On the possible choreography of the plays, see Wiles, *Greek Theatre Performance*, pp. 136-41.

**37**. Aristotle claimed (*Poetics* 6, 1450b18-20) that spectacle was the least integral element of the work, but this does not reflect the importance of spectacle to Athenian tragedy.

**38**. See Aristotle *Poetics* 4, 1449a9-14. On the origins of the genre of tragedy, unclear and much debated, see Lesky, *Greek Tragic Poetry*, pp. 1-24 and Csapo and Slater, *Context*, pp. 89-101.

**39**. On actors and acting, see Wiles, *Greek Theatre Performance*, pp. 147-64, Csapo and Slater, *Context*, pp. 221-55, and Easterling and Hall (eds), *Greek and Roman Actors*.

**40**. For a recent discussion on the Theatre of Dionysus and the many debates surrounding our understanding of its physical make-up, see ch. 2 in Wiles, *Tragedy in Athens*.

**41**. Blondell, *Sophocles' Antigone*, p. 6.

**42**. On the life of Sophocles, see Lesky, *Greek Tragic Poetry*, pp. 115-19.

**43**. *Poetics* 4, 1449a18-19.

**44**. See the *Life of Sophocles* section 4, found in Lefkowitz, *The Lives of the Greek Poets*, pp. 160-3. For the Greek, see Radt (ed.), *Tragicorum Graecorum Fragmenta*, vol. 4: *Sophocles*, pp. 29-41. See also Lefkowitz, pp. 75-87 for discussion of the biographical tradition on Sophocles, which is often of slight historical value.

**45**. About thirty of these plays were satyr plays, a sort of mythological farce. In the tragic competition the poet would present three tragedies with a single satyr play at the end. On the satyr play, see Seaford (ed.) *Euripides: Cyclops*, pp. 1-48. Note that three tragedians presented their work at a festival, chosen from a larger pool. Hence any drama that was performed at a festival was already, in this sense, a success.

**46**. The Sophists were travelling intellectuals who taught for pay a variety of subjects primarily to young men of the upper-classes. Many found success in Athens, despite the fact that they introduced new ideas to Athenian society which were often seen as incompatible with traditional values. For a contemporary picture of the Sophists, albeit of a humorous and stereotypical nature, see Aristophanes' *Clouds*. On the Sophists generally, see Kerferd, *The Sophistic Movement*.

**47**. Lesky, *Greek Tragic Poetry*, p. 193. For the perceived piety of Sophocles in ancient times, Lesky cites (p. 453, n. 6) the *Life of Sophocles*, section 12 (see Lefkowitz, *The Lives of the Greek Poets*, p. 161) and the scholion for Euripides' *Electra*, line 823 ('he was one of the most pious of men'). On more modern views of Sophoclean piety, see Lesky, *Greek Tragic Poetry*, pp. 192-5.

**48**. On the myth generally, see Jebb, *Commentary*, pp. x-xxiii, Kamerbeek, *Commentary*, pp. 1-7, Easterling, *Commentary*, pp. 415-19, March, *Creative Poet*, pp. 49-77 and Davies, *Commentary*, pp. xxii-xxxvii.

**49**. For the myths concerning Heracles, see Ganz, *Early Greek Myth*, pp. 374-466. For the extensive visual record of Heracles, see *Lexicon Iconographicum Mythologiae Classicae*, vol. 4.1, pp. 728-838, continued in vol. 5.1, pp. 1-196. For two stories of particular importance for the *Women of Trachis*, the battle between Heracles and Achelous, and the episode with Nessus, see vol. 1.1, pp. 25-8, and vol. 6.1, pp. 838-44 respectively.

**50**. For a good discussion of the foreknowledge of the audience and its limits, see Erp Taalman Kip, *Reader and Spectator*, ch. 2.

**51**. Burian, p. 179 in Easterling, *Cambridge Companion*.

**52**. An example of this sort of pairing is Achilles and Penthesilea in the epic cycle.

**53**. See March, *Creative Poet*, p. 54, Carawan, 'Deianeira's Guilt', p. 192.

**54**. The 'monstrosity' is the robe itself, now presumably already dyed in the water by the centaur's blood and the poison, and thus also the reason for the description of the Lycormas as 'rosy' (so Carawan, 'Deianeira's Guilt', pp. 199-200).

**55**. Carawan, 'Deianeira's Guilt', p. 198.

**56**. Compare Maehler, *Die Lieder des Bakchylides. Teil 2. Die Dithyramben und Fragmente*, p. 165: 'Fate makes use of her jealousy and her confused foresight to destroy not only Heracles but above all herself.'

**57**. In one of the Roman poet Ovid's (43 BC – AD 17) accounts of the story (*Metamorphoses* 9.1-272, the other being *Heroides* 9), Deianeira's first thought is in fact to kill Iole (149-51).

**58**. Garments in ancient Greece were somewhat 'unisex' (although they were worn in different manners), making such a gift possible. See Carawan, 'Deianeira's Guilt', p. 199 n. 33 for references.

**59**. Carawan, 'Deianeira's Guilt', pp. 200-1, also pp. 236-7 for the figures of the vase itself, and the cover of this book.

**60**. For magic used in love triangles to restrict (if not to kill) one's rival, see Faraone, *Ancient Greek Love Magic*, pp. 12-13.

**61**. Easterling, *Commentary*, pp. 19-23. For a detailed, but speculative and ultimately inconclusive study of the dating problem, see Hoey, 'The Date of the *Trachiniae*', pp. 210-32. Note also that we do not know whether the play won first prize.

**62**. Segal, *Tragic World*, p. 26.

**63**. A good example of the sorts of errors that can be made when works are dated by internal criteria, such as whether a work is 'primitive' or 'developed', is Aeschylus' *Suppliant Women*. This play, largely due to the dominance of the Chorus, had been widely considered to be an early work of the poet when a papyrus found in 1951 revealed that the play was in fact to be dated to Aeschylus' later career. See Jones, *On Aristotle and Greek Tragedy*, pp. 65-72 for discussion. On the issue of innovation and tradition more generally, see Michelini, *Tradition and Dramatic Form in the Persians of Aeschylus*, pp. 20-4.

**64**. See Heiden, *Rhetoric* and Kraus, 'Stories'.

**65**. Both the *Ajax* and the *Antigone* of Sophocles have a similar structure, and thus the three are often linked chronologically.

**66**. In particular 1051-2, spoken by Heracles, refers to the robe as 'a woven covering of the Furies', the specific phrasing of which closely recalls *Agamemnon* 1382 and 158. See Easterling, *Commentary*, pp. 21-2.

## 3. Plot

**1**. For a good account of the structure and effect of the plot, see Kamerbeek, *Commentary*, pp. 9-24.

**2**. Taplin, *The Stagecraft of Aeschylus*, p. 124. Burian, p. 188 in Easterling, *Cambridge Companion* also notes the element of a revenge tragedy, insofar as Nessus obtains his revenge by posthumously killing Heracles, although this is hardly the focus of the plot. See also Hall, pp. 107-9 in Easterling, *Cambridge Companion*, for a discussion of this type of plot structure.

**3**. The full extent of Heracles' reversal and downfall is succinctly described by Easterling, 'Sophocles, *Trachiniae*', p. 68: 'the greatest of men, the son of Zeus, is brought down in a particularly apt reversal in which the sacrificer becomes a victim, the monster-slayer is slain by monsters, the womaniser is enslaved by his passion for a woman and destroyed by the woman who loves him'.

**4**. Thus Seale, *Vision and Stagecraft*, p. 182.

**5**. On the theme of time in the play, see Segal, *Tragic World*, pp. 29-39 and ch. 3.

**6**. Thus the play has often been termed a 'diptych' (e.g. Webster, *An Introduction to Sophocles*, pp. 102-4.) See also Kirkwood, *Sophoclean Drama*, pp. 42-54 and Scodel, *Sophocles*, pp. 32-4. However, see Kane, 'Structure', for a good (if at times over-schematic) account of the play as having a three-part structure.

**7**. Seale, *Vision and Stagecraft*, pp. 201-2.

**8**. See Heath, *Unity in Greek Poetics*.

**9**. See Easterling, 'End of the Trachiniae', pp. 57-8.

**10**. On Athenian tragedy's ability to make use of generic expectations to produce such dissonance, see Burian, pp. 189-90 in Easterling, *Cambridge Companion*.

**11**. E.g. Clytemnestra's murder of her returning husband Agamemnon, in Aeschylus' *Agamemnon*, or Clytemnestra's death at the hands of the returning exile Orestes in the *Electra* plays of all three dramatists.

**12**. McCall, 'Structure, Focus and Heracles', p. 162 emphasises the fact that the same actor played the role of Heracles and of Deianeira, in this way creating continuity in the play.

**13**. See Kraus, 'Stories', for a discussion of how the characters of the play are continuously unable to come to final conclusions about the past and the stories they tell about it.

## 4. Character

**1**. *Poetics* 6, 1450a15-17: 'And the greatest of these (elements of drama) is the organisation of the events. For tragedy is not an imitation of people (as such), but of deeds and life'. This view has been defended influentially by Jones, *On Aristotle and Greek Tragedy*.

**2**. See Vernant, 'Intimations of the Will in Greek Tragedy' in Vernant and Vidal-Naquet, *Tragedy and Myth*, for a discussion of some of the differences in conceptions of character and agency between modern views and those that underlie Athenian tragedy.

**3**. See Blondell, *The Play of Character in Plato's Dialogues*, ch. 2.

**4**. For this viewpoint (sometimes called 'formalist', because characters are understood to be a product of the formal conditions of the literary work within which they exist), see Gould, 'Dramatic Character'.

**5**. For a good discussion of this point, see Easterling, 'Constructing Character in Greek Tragedy', pp. 83-99 in Pelling (ed.), *Characterization and Individuality in Greek Literature*.

**6**. On the similarities between the two women, see Segal, *Tragic World*, pp. 72-3.

**7**. See Zeitlin, p. 85 in Winkler and Zeitlin, *Nothing to Do with Dionysos*, for the self-reflective aspect of female characters in Athenian tragedy.

**8**. For the way that Deianeira in effect constructs Iole's character, see Wohl, *Intimate Commerce*, pp. 38-41.

**9**. For a good treatment of the theme of physical desire in the play, see Winnington-Ingram, *Sophocles*, ch. 4. See also Conacher, 'Sophocles' *Trachiniae*: Some Observations', for some important distinctions between the ways in which desire affects Deianeira and Heracles (pp. 29-31).

**10**. The Greek word (which literally means 'struggled for on both sides') recalls the battle of Heracles and Achelous for Deianeira. The point seems to be that whereas Deianeira was earlier the object of desire, it is now she who feels desire for another.

**11**. See Calame, *The Poetics of Eros in Ancient Greece*, pp. 120-1.

**12**. See Segal, *Tragedy and Civilization*, pp. 75-6 on the ambiguous status of Iole and the threat this represents to Deianeira.

**13**. The Furies were underworld, female goddesses of retribution, serving to punish primarily those who transgressed family bonds. On the role of concubines in Athenian tragedy, including their disruptive effects upon the family, see Foley, *Female Acts*, pp. 87-105. Compare also the statements concerning concubines and wives in Euripides' *Andromache* (e.g. 192-230, 461-501).

**14**. See Foley, *Female Acts*, pp. 88-9. The most important event in this development was Pericles' citizenship law of 451/0 BC (repassed in 403 BC), which made it a law that men could only produce legitimate children from citizen wives.

**15**. See Faraone, 'Deianeira's Mistake', and further Faraone, *Ancient Greek Love Magic*, pp. 110-19.

**16**. For Deianeira's guilt due to her lack of knowledge concerning the precise effects of the centaur's blood, see Carawan, 'Deianeira's Guilt', pp. 202-20.

**17**. For example, see Whitman, *Heroic Humanism*, pp. 112-13: 'The *Women of Trachis* is a love story.' Compared to Alcestis, Deianeira is 'quieter, nobler, and sweeter.' '... she is probably the only completely dignified picture of a passionately devoted woman extant in Greek Tragedy'. Compare also Jebb, *Commentary*, p. xxxi: 'The heroine of the *Trachiniae* has been recognised by general consent as one of the most delicately beautiful creations in literature.'

**18**. E.g. Faraone, 'Deianeira's Mistake', p. 115, Carawan, 'Deianeira's Guilt', p. 208.

**19**. Faraone, 'Deianeira's Mistake', pp. 120-3. Faraone softens his stance somewhat in his 1999 account ('desire might play some role', p. 118), although he maintains that desire is not essential to Deianeira's motivation.

**20**. See Rehm, *Marriage to Death*, p. 77.

**21**. See Loraux, *Tragic Ways of Killing a Woman*, pp. 7-30.

**22**. The paradigm of the affectionate marriage was that of Odysseus and Penelope in the *Odyssey*. See Foley, *Female Acts*, pp. 126-43.

**23**. Modern versions of this theory largely derive from Hegel and his explanation of the master-slave dialectic in the *Phenomenology of Spirit*, where the master desires that the slave *recognise* him as a master. However, the basic idea is not modern. The most explicit ancient account of such a view of desire I can cite is Ovid *Amores* II.19, where the poet complains that his mistress' husband is too lenient in watching over her, resulting in a cooling of Ovid's desire for the woman.

**24**. On slavery to sexual passion, see Davidson, *Courtesans and Fishcakes*, pp. 159-67.

**25**. This was a typical dilemma for women in Classical Athens: a 'good' woman was not supposed to have any independent reputation at all, in the sense of specific qualities or actions commented upon by others. A famous example of this view is found in the closing words of Pericles' funeral oration in Thucydides II.45.2: 'If I must say something of a woman's virtue to those who are now widowed, I can convey all with a brief piece of advice: your reputation will be great so long as you do not become less than your innate nature, and so long as there is the least mention among men of this nature, whether in praise or blame.'

**26**. See Wohl, *Intimate Commerce*, pp. 38-41.

**27**. See Ormand, *Exchange and the Maiden*, ch. 2 for Heracles' homosocial desire.

**28**. On the play's use of mythical monsters generally, see Sorum, 'Monsters'.

**29**. For a (perhaps overly) positive view of Heracles as the central heroic figure of the play, see McCall, 'Structure, Focus and Heracles', pp. 155-61.

**30**. On this central theme of wilderness and civilisation in the play, see Segal, *Tragedy and Civilization*, ch. 2.

**31**. See Easterling, 'Sophocles, *Trachiniae*', p. 65.

**32**. On the nature and function of heroes in Greek religion generally, see Burkert, *Greek Religion*, pp. 203-8. See also Kearns, *The Heroes of Attica*.

**33**. For Heracles in Greek religion, see Burkert, *Greek Religion*, pp. 208-11.

**34**. Segal, *Tragic World*, p. 53: 'the tragedy unfolds fully on the human plane with no supernatural solution to mitigate it, even though we are never allowed to forget the supernatural background.'

**35**. For various aspects of marriage ritual in the play, see Seaford, 'Wedding Ritual and Textual Criticism in Sophocles' "Women of Trachis"', pp. 50-9, and Segal, *Tragic World*, ch. 3.

**36**. Compare the death of Oedipus at the end of Sophocles' *Oedipus at Colonus*.

**37**. So Jebb, *Commentary*, p. xxxvii.

**38**. See Hall, pp. 109-10 in Easterling, *Cambridge Companion*.

**39**. Wohl, *Intimate Commerce*, p. 36, sees this as a good example of the way that Deianeira ultimately fails to occupy the role of either gender. On the gender reversals in the play generally, see Segal, *Tragedy and Civilization*, pp. 79-87.

**40**. Easterling, 'End of the *Trachiniae*', p. 58.

**41**. For good recent treatments, see Wohl, *Intimate Commerce*, ch. 1, Carawan, 'Deianeira's Guilt', pp. 220-3 and Pozzi, 'Hyllus' Coming of Age in Sophocles' *Trachiniae*' in Padilla (ed.), *Rites of Passage in Ancient Greece*.

**42**. In contrast, Sorum, 'Monsters', pp. 72-3 suggests that Hyllus' unwillingness to accede to Heracles' requests shows that he never truly leaves the sphere of his mother. On the relationship in general, see Strauss, *Fathers and Sons in Athens*.

**43**. On the various perversions that this union represents compared to usual Greek marriage practice, see Segal, *Tragic World*, pp. 86-7.

**44**. The relationship between psychoanalysis and literature has been a chequered one. See Brooks, *Psychoanalysis and Storytelling*, pp. 20-45. As Brooks discusses, the difficulties have in large part resulted from the fact that psychoanalysis has often tended to explain literature solely by its own precepts, without any concern for the principles that underlie the way that different forms of literature work. However, there are today both Classical scholars who use psychoanalytic theory to good result (for example, see Wohl, *Intimate Commerce*) and psycho-analytic scholars who read tragedy non-reductively (for example, see Alford, *The Psychoanalytic Theory of Greek Tragedy*).

**45**. But note that the Nurse's account of Hyllus when he discovered Deianeira dead, describing how he 'threw himself down by her side' (948-9), will be echoed by Heracles' demand of Hyllus that no one else possess Iole who 'lay by my side' (1225-6), in particular because in Greek the notion of placing side by side has sexual connotations to it. See Foley, *Female Acts*, p. 97.

**46**. Pomeroy, *Families*, p. 23. Note that this does not mean that the re-establishment of the family at the end of the play is simply positive in value. Foley, 'The Conception of Women in Athenian Drama' in her (ed.) *Reflections of Women in Antiquity*, p. 159: 'We are left with a feeling that cultured order has been recreated at too high a price.'

## 5. Performance

**1**. See Heath, *The Poetics of Greek Tragedy*, on the importance of the emotional aspect of Athenian tragedy.

**2**. For a full examination of the dramatic staging of the play, see Seale's chapter on the *Women of Trachis*, to which my account here is indebted on many points.

**3**. See Easterling, *Commentary*, p. 104.

**4**. See Kamerbeek, *Commentary*, p. 13: 'The song with its swift movement is in marked contrast with the opening of the next scene: the mournful train of weeping captives slowly drawing near. In this respect few transitions in Greek Tragedy are comparable'. However, I would not see the captives as 'weeping', although having the joyous song of one group overwhelmed by the lamentation of another would have its own dramatic impact.

**5**. See Seale, *Vision and Stagecraft*, pp. 188-9 for some of the different ways this contrast might have been expressed in performance.

**6**. Seale, *Vision and Stagecraft*, p. 195.

**7**. This can be described as 'dramatic irony', in that the audience knows something (here the identity of Iole) which one of the characters (Deianeira) does not. For a good discussion of dramatic irony, see Erp Taalman Kip, *Reader and Spectator*, ch. 4.

**8**. Hester, 'Deianeira's "Deception Speech"', pp. 1-8 argues that the whole purpose of Deianeira's speech at 436-69, when she expresses her acceptance of Heracles' desire for Iole, is to reveal the irony that Deianeira does not in fact reflect her epic version as a vengeful and deliberate killer of her husband.

**9**. Compare Heiden, *Rhetoric*, p. 74: 'Yet in averring that love does rule her [...] Deianeira discloses the passion that her rhetoric seeks to suppress.'

**10**. Erp Taalman Kip, *Reader and Spectator*, pp. 81-4, usefully describes this sort of effect as dramatic irony based on superior judgement, rather than on superior knowledge: that is, the audience finds the choral song ironic not because they definitely know (unlike the Chorus) that Deianeira will react in a violent fashion due to the influence of *erôs*, but because they can judge her, based on her own previous statements, as liable to act in such a way. This suspicion produces a rupture between the ode's surface meaning and a second, more anxious, meaning.

**11**. Winnington-Ingram, *Sophocles*, p. 78: 'The less characteristic the act, then the greater is the evidence of her desperation.'

## 6. Theme

**1**. See Wohl, *Intimate Commerce*, pp. xviii-xxiv for a recent discussion.

**2**. See Zeitlin, pp. 130-67 in Winkler and Zeitlin, *Nothing to Do with Dionysos*. Zeitlin argues that the city of Thebes is used as an 'anti-Athens', as a safe location for investigations into Athenian questions and problems. The *Women of Trachis*, dealing as it does with Heracles, another famous figure of Thebes (although the play is not set in Thebes), arguably fits within her paradigm (see Zeitlin, p. 144 n. 16).

**3**. See Ormand, *Exchange and the Maiden*, pp. 42-3, 50.

**4**. *Sôphrosunê* was also a virtue for the good woman (see the description of the bee woman in Semonides 7), but we have seen that the ideological type that Deianeira is constructed upon is that of the vengeful, destructive, wife.

**5**. See Foley, *Female Acts*, pp. 89-90 for discussion and references.

**6**. Hall, pp. 121-2 in Easterling, *Cambridge Companion*, notes that in all three of our extant tragedies which depict a man bringing home a concubine to be established in the home (*Women of Trachis*, Aeschylus' *Agamemnon* and Euripides' *Andromache*), the man is destroyed by his wife.

**7**. Similarly, Patterson, 'Marriage in Athenian Law' in Pomeroy (ed.), *Women's History and Ancient History*, p. 57, suggests that the *Women of Trachis* 'may in fact show that despite the relative sexual freedom of Greek men (and especially Heracles), marriage was quite clearly and unambiguously understood in Athens to be properly a singular relation which linked (or yoked) two people, one husband and one wife'.

**8**. For one of the more famous examples of the maxim, see Herodotus' account of Solon and Croesus, 1.30-3 and 86.

**9**. For good treatments of the theme, see Whitman, *Heroic Humanism*, ch. 6, Lawrence, 'Dramatic Epistemology', and Scodel, *Sophocles*, ch. 3.

**10**. On this irony, see Whitman, *Heroic Humanism*, pp. 110-11.

**11**. See Heiden, *Rhetoric* and Segal, *Tragedy and Civilization*, pp. 93-8 for the play's depiction of the failure of language.

**12**. See L. Bowman, 'Prophecy and Authority in the *Trachiniai*', pp. 335-50. Note that in the *Hercules Oetaeus* attributed to Seneca (for discussion, see below, pp. 118-19), Heracles is only able to meet his impending death when he learns of the involvement of Nessus (1396), because this means for him that he has not truly been bested by a women, but by one of the savage creatures he previously vanquished.

**13**. See Segal, *Tragedy and Civilization*, pp. 101-2. In Pound's version of the play (see below, pp. 119-20), Heracles' recognition of the truth of the oracles is the core of the play, as indicated by his removing his 'tragic' mask (Pound, *Women of Trachis*, pp. 66-7).

**14**. On this parallel, see Sorum, 'Monsters', p. 68.

**15**. Segal, *Tragic World*, pp. 51-2.

**16**. Compare Euripides' *Hercules Furens*.

**17**. See Williams, '*The Women of Trachis*: Fictions, Pessimism, Ethics', in Louden and Schollmeier (eds), *The Greeks and Us*, for a challenging but interesting philosophical study of the pessimism of the play, suggesting (after Nietzsche) that such depictions of suffering allow the spectator to clearly examine the cruelty of the world without being personally overcome by it. Similar is the final assessment of Segal, *Tragic World*, pp. 64-5: the piety of the play 'is far less a confident religiosity or a consoling faith than the strength to face the darkness of the universe, the mystery of evil, and to recognise that the equilibrating forces of the world may not be totally congruent with human purposes or human ideas of justice and order'.

**18**. Bruce Heiden, *Rhetoric*, p. 147 goes so far as to suggest that the oracles at the end of the play are not so much found to be true, as Heracles *makes* them true by his interpretation of them, and by his decision to kill himself. Heracles acts in accordance with what he thinks the oracles mean in order to thereby prove them true.

**19**. For a different emphasis on Heracles' sense of knowledge derived from the oracles and his fate, see Segal, *Tragic World*, pp. 47-55, who argues that his final lines 'show the possibility that this rude hero can be purged of the bestiality with which he has struggled all his life' (54).

**20**. Zeitlin, p. 78 in Winkler and Zeitlin, *Nothing to Do with Dionysos*.

**21**. On Zeus in Greek religion, see Burkert, *Greek Religion*, pp. 125-31.

**22**. Zeus is referred to over thirty times in the play, both by virtue of his being the father of Heracles and otherwise.

**23**. Compare 26-7, 126-31, 200-1, 303-5, 983-6, 1000-2, 1159-61, 1278.

**24**. Easterling, *Commentary*, p. 91.

**25**. See Lloyd-Jones, *Justice of Zeus*, pp. 104-28.

**26**. Lloyd-Jones, *Justice of Zeus*, p.128: '*Dikê* means not only "justice", but "the order of the universe", and from the human point of view that order often seems to impose a natural rather than a moral law.'

**27**. On oracles, see Burkert, *Greek Religion*, pp. 114-18.

**28**. See Holt, 'The End of the *Trachiniai*', pp. 70-2, for a good summary of the main points. For the older view that Heracles was simply mortal, see *Odyssey* 11, where Odysseus in Hades sees Heracles, who is precisely presented as an example of how all men, even one born of Zeus, are subject to death.

**29**. This point is central to Stinton's detailed argument that the play does not contain an allusion to the apotheosis ('The Scope and Limits of Allusion in Greek Tragedy' in Cropp et al. (eds) *Greek Tragedy and its Legacy*, pp. 67-102). However, to work from an assumption about what the final dramatic effect of the play *should* be is to work backwards.

**30**. Finkelberg, 'Second Stasimon', pp. 130-9.

**31**. Holt, 'The End of the *Trachiniae*', drawing on past scholarship on the issue, summarises the arguments and makes a strong case for there being an allusion to the apotheosis.

**32**. See Finkelberg, 'Second Stasimon', pp. 139-43. Lawrence, 'Dramatic Epistemology', p. 291, remarked earlier that the oracle, if understood as signifying a choice between death or death, is 'grossly deceptive'.

**33**. Those, like Segal, *Tragic World*, p. 53, who do accept the allusion to the apotheosis tend to emphasise that the human characters do not know of Heracles' fate, and therefore that there is no lessening of the tragic effect at the end. Johansen, 'Heracles in Sophocles' *Trachiniae*', pp. 47-61 also saw this matter in a positive light, suggesting that by including the allusion to the apotheosis, 'Sophocles gave himself the opportunity of posing with particular poignancy and brutality the question of the interplay and lack of understanding between god and man' (p. 60).

**34**. See Lloyd-Jones, *Justice of Zeus*, pp. 126-8.

**35**. Finkelberg, 'Second Stasimon', p. 140.

**36**. Xenophanes fr. 11 famously mocks the anthropomorphism of Greek religion: 'But if cattle and horses or lions had hands, or wrote with their hands and performed deeds which humans perform, horses would draw the forms of the gods like horses and cattle like cattle, and they would make (the gods') bodies like the body each had themselves.' For Herodotus' discussion of Heracles, see Herodotus 2.43-5. It should also be noted that criticism of myth was itself an accepted practice. See Parker, *Athenian Religion*, p. 203.

**37**. Finkelberg, 'Second Stasimon', p. 143. Roberts, 'Sophoclean Endings', pp. 188-9 suggests that all of the endings of Sophocles' extant corpus are ironic in this way.

**38**. So Erp Taalman Kip, *Reader and Spectator*, pp. 86-7.

**39**. For a view of the ending of the play as ambiguous, see Hoey, 'Ambiguity in the Exodos of Sophocles' *Trachiniae*', pp. 269-94.

**40**. Roberts, 'Sophoclean Endings', p. 191.

**41**. This process has been described by the hermeneutic philosopher Hans-Georg Gadamer, *Truth and Method*, as a 'fusion of horizons'.

# 7. Reception

**1**. See Jauss, *Toward an Aesthetic of Reception*.

**2**. For a general introduction to the reception of Athenian drama, see Wiles, *Greek Theatre Performance*, ch. 8. For Athenian tragedy in general, the most influential such reception has been Aristotle's *Poetics*: to this day, over two thousand years later, one is still likely to hear that a good tragedy should possess a unified plot. Similarly, it is today impossible to read Sophocles' *Oedipus Rex* without being influenced by Freud's famous reception of that play. On Aristotle's *Poetics* and its influence (often based on misinterpretations of Aristotle's meaning), see Jones, *On Aristotle and Greek Tragedy*, pp. 11-62. For a (critical) view of the 'Oedipus complex' from a classicist's position, see Vernant, 'Oedipus without the Complex' in Vernant and Vidal-Naquet, *Tragedy and Myth*.

**3**. See Galinsky, *Herakles*, p. 2.

**4**. See Xenophon *Memorabilia* 2.1.29-34 for the famous 'Choice of Heracles', a myth attributed to the fifth-century intellectual and educator Prodicus relating how Virtue and Vice personified came to the hero in an attempt to win him over to their respective ways of life. See Galinsky, *Herakles*, pp. 101-3 for discussion.

**5**. As Galinsky, *Herakles*, p. 81, notes, in ancient Greece Heracles was in fact most popular on the comic stage. See, for example, Heracles' portrayal in Aristophanes' *Frogs* 38-164.

**6**. See Dawe, *Heritage*, for a look at some receptions of Sophocles in general (in which the *Women of Trachis* does not figure prominently). Flashar, *Inszenierung*, p. 240, notes that the play is rarely restaged, and when it is it is typically Pound's version that is used (see further below). Similarly, Hartigan, *Greek Tragedy on the American Stage*, p. 138 notes only one commercial performance of the play in America (a production of Pound's adaptation).

**7**. 'Hercules' is the Latin form of the Greek name Heracles. 'Oetaeus' means 'of Oeta', and is used to specify which part of Heracles' story the play deals with.

**8**. On the relationship between *Heroides* IX and previous versions of the myth, and in particular with the *Women of Trachis*, see Jacobson, *Ovid's Heroides*, pp. 235-8.

**9**. This refers to Heracles' enslavement to Omphale (cf. *Women of Trachis* 69-70, 248-53), which was often portrayed in comic treatments as it is in *Heroides* IX (53-118), with Heracles being presented as dressed in women's clothing and made to perform tasks traditionally assigned to women.

**10**. See Jacobsen, *Ovid's Heroides*, pp. 238-40.

**11**. On Stoicism and Senecan tragedy, see Rosenmeyer, *Senecan Drama and Stoic Cosmology*. On the *Hercules Oetaeus* specifically, see Galinsky, *Herakles*, pp. 174-81. Note that today the play is generally not considered to have been written by Seneca.

**12**. Seneca's own 'Stoic' suicide is described in Tacitus *Annals* 15.60-4.

**13**. Pound's knowledge of Greek was not all that strong. On his translation of the *Women of Trachis*, see Ingber, 'Ezra Pound's Women of Trachis', pp. 240-4, and Xie, 'Pound as translator', pp. 214-17 in Nadel (ed.), *The Cambridge Companion to Ezra Pound*.

**14**. See Easterling, *Commentary*, p. 165.

**15**. This understanding of Heracles was in turn connected to Pound's view that the *Women of Trachis* was of all extant Athenian tragedies the most similar to Japanese Noh drama. See Ingber, 'Ezra Pound's Women of Trachis', pp. 138-44.

**16**. This account of Heyme production is taken from Flashar, *Inszenierung*, pp. 240-1.

# Further Reading

## Historical and cultural background

W. Burkert, *Greek Religion*, trans. John Raffan. (Cambridge, Massachusetts: Harvard University Press, 1985) (original German edition 1977). An excellent overview.

E. Csapo and W.J. Slater, *The Context of Ancient Greek Drama* (Ann Arbor: University of Michigan Press, 1994). Collects all the evidence on ancient drama and performance.

A. Maria van Erp Taalman Kip, *Reader and Spectator: Problems in the Interpretation of Greek Tragedy* (Amsterdam: J.C. Gieben, 1990). Lucid treatments of some important issues in the interpretation of drama.

G.K. Galinsky, *The Herakles Theme: The Adaptations of the Hero in Literature from Homer to the Twentieth Century* (Oxford: Blackwell, 1972). The reception of Heracles through the centuries.

J. Gould, 'Law, Custom and Myth: Aspects of the Social Position of Women in Classical Athens', *Journal of Hellenic Studies* 100 (1980), pp. 38-59.

H. Lloyd-Jones, *The Justice of Zeus* (2nd ed.) (Berkeley: University of California Press, 1983). An influential study.

J.R. March, *The Creative Poet: Studies on the Treatment of Myths in Greek Poetry* (London: University of London, Institute of Classical Studies, 1987). A good treatment of Sophocles' use of previous accounts of the myth.

J. Ober, *Mass and Elite in Democratic Athens: Rhetoric, Ideology, and the Power of the People* (Princeton: Princeton University Press, 1989). Power and perception in the democracy.

A. Pickard-Cambridge, *The Dramatic Festivals of Athens*, 2nd ed. revised by J. Gould and D.M. Lewis (Oxford: Clarendon Press, 1968). Standard starting point for the festivals.

S.B. Pomeroy, *Families in Classical and Hellenistic Greece: Representations and Realities* (Oxford: Clarendon Press, 1997).

J.J. Winkler and F. Zeitlin (eds), *Nothing to Do with Dionysos? Athenian Drama in its Social Context* (Princeton: Princeton University Press, 1990). A highly influential collection of essays.

## Further Reading

## Athenian tragedy

P.E. Easterling (ed.), *The Cambridge Companion to Greek Tragedy* (Cambridge: Cambridge University Press, 1997). An excellent new introduction.

H.P. Foley, *Female Acts in Greek Tragedy* (Princeton and Oxford: Princeton University Press, 2001). An important new book drawing on feminist theory.

C. Garton, 'Characterisation in Greek Tragedy', *Journal of Hellenic Studies* 77 (1957), pp. 247-54. A good general account of the topic.

S. Goldhill, *Reading Greek Tragedy* (Cambridge: Cambridge University Press, 1986). A more theoretical introduction to Athenian tragedy.

J. Gould, 'Dramatic Character and Human Intelligibility in Greek Tragedy', *Proceedings of the Cambridge Philological Society* 24 (1978), pp. 43-67. A very influential study of character.

J. Jones, *On Aristotle and Greek Tragedy* (Stanford: Stanford University Press, 1962). Argues against the centrality of character in Athenian tragedy.

A. Lesky, *Greek Tragic Poetry*, trans. M. Dillon (New Haven and London: Yale University Press, 1983) (original German edition: 1972). A useful overview of Greek tragedy.

O. Taplin, *Greek Tragedy in Action* (London: Methuen, 1978). A highly influential study of performance in Athenian tragedy.

D. Wiles, *Greek Theatre Performance: An Introduction* (Cambridge: Cambridge University Press, 2000). A good recent introduction to the contexts and performance of Athenian tragedy.

J-P. Vernant and P. Vidal-Naquet. *Tragedy and Myth in Ancient Greece*, trans. Janet Lloyd (Sussex and New Jersey: Harvester Press and Humanities Press, 1981) (original French publication: 1972). Collection of essays by two influential structuralists.

V. Wohl, *Intimate Commerce: Exchange, Gender, and Subjectivity in Greek Tragedy* (Austin: University of Texas Press, 1998). Good use of contemporary theory.

## Sophocles

R.D. Dawe (ed.), *Sophocles: The Classical Heritage* (New York and London: Garland Publishing, 1996). A collection of historical essays on the reception of Sophocles.

G.M. Kirkwood, *A Study of Sophoclean Drama* (Ithaca and London: Cornell University Press, 1958). A useful account of Sophoclean drama by artistic element.

K. Ormand, *Exchange and the Maiden: Marriage in Sophoclean*

*Tragedy* (Austin: University of Texas Press, 1999). A stimulating treatment of the play.

R. Scodel, *Sophocles* (Boston: Twayne, 1984). Accessible and engaging.

D. Seale, *Vision and Stagecraft in Sophocles* (Chicago: University of Chicago Press, 1982). An examination of the visual and theatrical aspects of Sophocles.

C. Segal, *Tragedy and Civilization: An Interpretation of Sophocles* (Cambridge, Massachusetts and London: Harvard University Press, 1981). A structuralist reading by an important interpreter of the play.

C. Segal, *Sophocles' Tragic World: Divinity, Nature, Society* (Cambridge and London: Harvard University Press, 1995). Collection of essays.

C.H. Whitman, *Sophocles: A Study of Heroic Humanism* (Cambridge, Massachusetts: Harvard University Press, 1966). Good on theme of late-learning.

R.P. Winnington-Ingram, *Sophocles: An Interpretation* (Cambridge: Cambridge University Press, 1980). An important study, especially good on the role of desire in the play.

## Women of Trachis

### Commentaries

Note that one does not need to be able to read Greek to make use of language commentaries, as they regularly contain valuable points of interpretation.

M. Davies (ed.), *Sophocles: Trachiniae* (Oxford: Clarendon Press, 1991). Scholarly edition.

P.E. Easterling (ed.), *Sophocles: Trachiniae* (Cambridge: Cambridge University Press, 1982). A highly useful modern commentary.

R.C. Jebb (ed.), *Sophocles The Plays and Fragments. Part V: The Trachiniae* (Cambridge: Cambridge University Press, 1892; reprinted with new Introductions by P.E. Easterling and Barbara Goward: London: Bristol Classical Press, 2004). Still very valuable.

J.C. Kamerbeek (ed.), *The Plays of Sophocles: II. The Trachiniae* (Leiden: Brill, 1959). Contains a good literary introduction.

### Translations

D. Grene and R. Lattimore (eds), *The Complete Greek Tragedies: Sophocles II* (Chicago: University of Chicago Press, 1957). *Women of Trachis.* Translator: Michael Jameson

# Further Reading

H. Lloyd-Jones (ed. and trans.), Sophocles II (Cambridge, Massachusetts: Harvard University Press, 1994). A good literal translation of the play.

E. Pound (trans.), *Sophocles: Women of Trachis* (London: Faber and Faber, 1969).

C.K. Williams and G.W. Dickerson (trans.), *Sophocles: Women of Trachis* (New York and Oxford: Oxford University Press, 1978). Free but forceful translation by poet-scholar team.

## *Studies*

E. Carawan, 'Deianeira's Guilt', *Transactions of the American Philological Association* 130 (2000), pp. 189-237. Reassesses earlier mythic treatments of Deianeira.

P.E. Easterling, 'Sophocles, Trachiniae', *Bulletin of the Institute of Classical Studies* 16 (1968), pp. 58-69. Important study for the play's recent revival.

P.E. Easterling, 'The End of the *Trachiniae*', *Illinois Classical Studies* 6 (1981), pp. 56-74.

C.A. Faraone, 'Deianeira's Mistake and the Demise of Heracles: Erotic Magic in Sophocles' *Women of Trachis*', *Helios* 21 (1994), pp. 115-35. Important contribution to our understanding of Deianeira's motivation.

M. Finkelberg, 'The Second Stasimon of the *Trachiniae* and Heracles' Festival on Mount Oeta', *Mnemosyne* 49 (1996), pp. 129-43. Recent look at the apotheosis.

B. Heiden, *Tragic Rhetoric: An Interpretation of Sophocles'* Trachiniae (New York: Peter Lang, 1989). Literary commentary on the play's use of ambiguous language.

P. Holt, 'The End of the *Trachiniai* and the Fate of Herakles', *Journal of Hellenic Studies* 109 (1989), pp. 69-80. Makes a strong argument for there being an allusion to the apotheosis.

R.L. Kane, 'The Structure of Sophocles' *Trachiniae*: "Diptych" or "Trilogy"?', *Phoenix* 42 (1988), pp. 198-211. Novel examination of the structure of the plot.

C.S. Kraus, 'LOGOS MEN EST' ARKHAIOS: Stories and Story-telling in Sophocles' *Trachiniae*', *Transactions of the American Philological Association* 121 (1991), pp. 75-98. Examines the importance of narrative in the play.

S.E. Lawrence, 'The Dramatic Epistemology of Sophocles' *Trachiniae*', *Phoenix* 32 (1978), pp. 288-304. A good examination of the theme of knowledge.

M. McCall, 'The *Trachiniae*: Structure, Focus and Heracles', *American Journal of Philology* 93 (1972), pp. 142-63

D.H. Roberts, 'Sophoclean Endings: Another Story', *Arethusa* 21 (1988), 177-96. Ambiguity in the endings of Sophocles' plays.

C.E. Sorum, 'Monsters and the Family: the Exodos of Sophocles' *Trachiniae*', *Greek, Roman and Byzantine Studies* 19 (1978), 59-73.

# Bibliography

C.F. Alford, *The Psychoanalytic Theory of Greek Tragedy* (New Haven and London: Yale University Press, 1992).

E. Belfiore, 'Problematic Reciprocity in Greek Tragedy', pp. 139-58 in C. Gill et al. (eds). *Reciprocity in Ancient Greece* (Oxford: Oxford University Press, 1998).

R. Blondell, *Sophocles' Antigone* (Newburyport, Massachusetts: Focus, 1998).

────── *The Play of Character in Plato's Dialogues* (Cambridge: Cambridge University Press, 2002).

M.W. Blundell, *Helping Friends and Harming Enemies: A Study in Sophocles and Greek Ethics* (Cambridge and New York: Cambridge University Press, 1989).

P. Bourdieu, *The Rules of Art: Genesis and Structure of the Literary Field*, trans. Susan Emanuel (Stanford: Stanford University Press, 1995).

L. Bowman, 'Prophecy and Authority in the *Trachiniai*', *American Journal of Philology* 120 (1999), pp. 335-50.

P. Brooks, *Psychoanalysis and Storytelling* (Oxford: Blackwell, 1994).

W. Burkert, *Greek Religion*, trans. John Raffan (Cambridge, Massachusetts: Harvard University Press, 1985; original German edition 1977).

R.W.B. Burton, *The Chorus in Sophocles' Tragedies* (Oxford: Oxford University Press, 1980).

D.L. Cairns, *Aidos: The Psychology and Ethics of Honour and Shame in Ancient Greek Literature* (Oxford: Clarendon Press, 1993).

C. Calame, *The Poetics of Eros in Ancient Greece*, trans. J. Lloyd (Princeton: Princeton University Press, 1999).

E. Carawan, 'Deianeira's Guilt', *Transactions of the American Philological Association* 130 (2000), pp. 189-237.

D.J. Conacher, 'Sophocles' *Trachiniae*: Some Observations', *American Journal of Philology* 118 (1997), pp. 21-33.

E. Csapo and W.J. Slater, *The Context of Ancient Greek Drama* (Ann Arbor: University of Michigan Press, 1994).

J. Davidson, *Courtesans and Fishcakes: The Consuming Passions of Classical Athens* (New York: St Martin's Press, 1997).

M. Davies (ed.), *Sophocles: Trachiniae* (Oxford: Clarendon Press, 1991).

R.D. Dawe (ed.), *Sophocles: The Classical Heritage* (New York and London: Garland Publishing, 1996).

P.E. Easterling, 'Sophocles, *Trachiniae*', *Bulletin of the Institute of Classical Studies* 16 (1968), pp. 58-69.

────── 'The End of the *Trachiniae*', *Illinois Classical Studies* 6 (1981), pp. 56-74.

────── (ed.) *Sophocles: Trachiniae* (Cambridge: Cambridge University Press, 1982).

────── 'Constructing Character in Greek Tragedy', pp. 83-99 in C. Pelling (ed.), *Characterization and Individuality in Greek Literature* (Oxford: Clarendon Press, 1990).

────── *The Cambridge Companion to Greek Tragedy* (Cambridge: Cambridge University Press, 1997).

P.E. Easterling and E. Hall (eds), *Greek and Roman Actors: Aspects of an Ancient Profession* (Cambridge: Cambridge University Press, 2002).

A. Maria van Erp Taalman Kip, *Reader and Spectator: Problems in the Interpretation of Greek Tragedy* (Amsterdam: J.C. Gieben, 1990).

C.A. Faraone, 'Deianeira's Mistake and the Demise of Heracles: Erotic Magic in Sophocles' *Women of Trachis*', *Helios* 21 (1994), pp. 115-35.

────── *Ancient Greek Love Magic* (Cambridge, Massachusetts: Harvard University Press, 1999).

M. Finkelberg, 'The Second Stasimon of the *Trachiniae* and Heracles' Festival on Mount Oeta', *Mnemosyne* 49 (1996), pp. 129-43.

H. Flashar, *Inszenierung der Antike: Das griechische Drama auf der Bühne der Neuzeit 1585-1990* (München: Beck, 1991).

H.P. Foley (ed.), *Reflections of Women in Antiquity* (New York, London and Paris: Gordon and Breach Science Publishers, 1981).

────── *Female Acts in Greek Tragedy* (Princeton and Oxford: Princeton University Press, 2001).

C. Fornara and L. Samons, *Athens from Cleisthenes to Pericles* (Berkeley: University of California Press, 1991).

H-G. Gadamer, *Truth and Method*, trans. Joel Weinsheimer and Donald G. Marshall, 2nd ed. (New York: Continuum, 1999; original German publication, 1960).

G.K. Galinsky, *The Herakles Theme: The Adaptations of the Hero in Literature from Homer to the Twentieth Century* (Oxford: Blackwell, 1972).

T. Ganz, *Early Greek Myth: A Guide to the Literary and Artistic Sources* (Baltimore and London: John Hopkins Press, 1993).

C. Garton, 'Characterisation in Greek Tragedy', *Journal of Hellenic Studies* 77 (1957), pp. 247-54.

B. Goff (ed.), *History, Tragedy, Theory: Dialogues on Athenian Drama* (Austin: University of Texas Press, 1995).

# Bibliography

S. Goldhill, *Reading Greek Tragedy* (Cambridge: Cambridge University Press, 1986).

J. Gould, 'Dramatic Character and Human Intelligibility in Greek Tragedy', *Proceedings of the Cambridge Philological Society* 24 (1978), pp. 43-67.

────── 'Law, Custom and Myth: Aspects of the Social Position of Women in Classical Athens', *Journal of Hellenic Studies* 100 (1980), pp. 38-59.

────── 'Tragedy and Collective Experience', pp. 217-43 in M.S. Silk (ed.), *Tragedy and the Tragic: Greek Theatre and Beyond* (Oxford: Clarendon Press, 1996).

D. Grene and R. Lattimore (eds), *The Complete Greek Tragedies: Sophocles II* (Chicago: University of Chicago Press, 1957).

M. Hansen, *Democracy and Demography: The Number of Athenian Citizens in the Fourth Century BC* (Herning: Systime, 1986).

K.V. Hartigan, *Greek Tragedy on the American Stage: Ancient Drama in the Commercial Theatre, 1882-1994* (Westport, Connecticut and London: Greenwood Press, 1995).

M. Heath, *The Poetics of Greek Tragedy* (Stanford: Stanford University Press and London: Duckworth, 1987).

────── *Unity in Greek Poetics* (Oxford: Clarendon Press, 1989).

B. Heiden, *Tragic Rhetoric: An Interpretation of Sophocles'* Trachiniae (New York: Peter Lang, 1989).

D.A. Hester, 'Deianeira's "Deception Speech" ', *Antichthon* 14 (1980), pp. 1-8.

T.F. Hocy, 'Ambiguity in the Exodos of Sophocles' *Trachiniae*', *Arethusa* 10 (1977), pp. 269-94.

P. Holt, 'The End of the *Trachiniai* and the Fate of Herakles', *Journal of Hellenic Studies* 109 (1989), pp. 69-80.

R. Ingber, 'Ezra Pound's Women of Trachis: A Song for the Muses' Garden', *Amerikastudien* 23 (1978), pp. 131-46.

H. Jacobson, *Ovid's Heroides* (Princeton: Princeton University Press, 1974).

H.R. Jauss, *Toward an Aesthetic of Reception*, trans. Timothy Bahti (Minneapolis: University of Minnesota Press, 1982).

R.C. Jebb (ed.), *Sophocles The Plays and Fragments. Part V: The Trachiniae* (Cambridge: Cambridge University Press, 1892; reprinted with new Introductions by P.E. Easterling and Barbara Goward: London: Bristol Classical Press, 2004).

H.F. Johansen, 'Heracles in Sophocles' *Trachiniae*', *Classica et Mediaevalia* 37 (1986), pp. 47-61

J. Jones, *On Aristotle and Greek Tragedy* (Stanford: Stanford University Press, 1962).

J.C. Kamerbeek (ed.), *The Plays of Sophocles: II. The Trachiniae* (Leiden: Brill, 1959).

R.L. Kane, 'The Structure of Sophocles' *Trachiniae*: "Diptych" or "Trilogy"?', *Phoenix* 42 (1988), pp. 198-211.

E. Kearns, *The Heroes of Attica, Bulletin of the Institute of Classical Studies* Suppl. 57 (London: University of London, 1989).

G. Kerferd, *The Sophistic Movement* (Cambridge: Cambridge University Press, 1981).

G.M. Kirkwood, *A Study of Sophoclean Drama* (Ithaca and London: Cornell University Press, 1958).

B. Knox, *The Heroic Temper: Studies in Sophoclean Tragedy* (Berkeley: University of California, 1964).

C.S. Kraus, 'LOGOS MEN EST' ARKHAIOS: Stories and Story-telling in Sophocles' *Trachiniae*', *Transactions of the American Philological Association* 121 (1991), pp. 75-98.

S.E. Lawrence, 'The Dramatic Epistemology of Sophocles' *Trachiniae*', *Phoenix* 32 (1978), pp. 288-304.

M.R. Lefkowitz, *The Lives of the Greek Poets* (Baltimore: John Hopkins University Press, 1981).

A. Lesky, *Greek Tragic Poetry*, trans. M. Dillon (New Haven and London: Yale University Press, 1983; original German edition, 1972).

*Lexicon Iconographicum Mythologiae Classicae* (Zurich: Artemis, 1981-1999).

H. Lloyd-Jones, *The Justice of Zeus*, 2nd ed. (Berkeley: University of California Press, 1983).

——— (ed. and trans.), *Sophocles II* (Cambridge, Massachusetts: Harvard University Press, 1994).

N. Loraux, *Tragic Ways of Killing a Woman*, trans. A. Forester (Cambridge, Massachusetts and London: Harvard University Press, 1987).

H. Maehler (ed.), *Die Lieder des Bakchylides. Teil 2. Die Dithyramben und Fragmente: Text, Übersetzung und Kommentar* (Leiden: Brill, 1997).

P.B. Manville, *The Origins of Citizenship in Ancient Athens* (Princeton: Princeton University Press, 1990).

J.R. March, *The Creative Poet: Studies on the Treatment of Myths in Greek Poetry* (London: University of London, Institute of Classical Studies, 1987).

M. McCall, 'The *Trachiniae*: Structure, Focus and Heracles', *American Journal of Philology* 93 (1972), pp. 142-63.

A.N. Michelini, *Tradition and Dramatic Form in the Persians of Aeschylus* (Leiden: E.J. Brill, 1982).

L.G. Mitchell, *Greeks Bearing Gifts: The Public Use of Private*

*Relationships in the Greek World, 435-323 BC* (Cambridge: Cambridge University Press).

J. Ober, *Mass and Elite in Democratic Athens: Rhetoric, Ideology, and the Power of the People* (Princeton: Princeton University Press, 1989).

K. Ormand, *Exchange and the Maiden: Marriage in Sophoclean Tragedy* (Austin: University of Texas Press, 1999).

R. Parker, *Athenian Religion: A History* (Oxford: Clarendon Press, 1996).

C. Pelling (ed.), *Greek Tragedy and the Historian* (Oxford: Clarendon Press, 1997).

A. Pickard-Cambridge, *The Dramatic Festivals of Athens*, 2nd ed. revised by J. Gould and D.M. Lewis (Oxford: Clarendon Press, 1968).

S.B. Pomeroy (ed.), *Women's History and Ancient History* (Chapel Hill and London: University of North Carolina Press, 1991).

—— *Families in Classical and Hellenistic Greece: Representations and Realities* (Oxford: Clarendon Press, 1997).

E. Pound (trans.), *Sophocles: Women of Trachis* (London: Faber and Faber, 1969). Referred to in this book by page number.

D.C. Pozzi, 'Hyllus' Coming of Age in Sophocles' *Trachiniae'*, pp. 29-41 in M.W. Padilla (ed.), *Rites of Passage in Ancient Greece* (Lewisburg, London and Toronto: Bucknell University Press and Associated University Presses, 1999).

S. Radt (ed.), *Tragicorum Graecorum Fragmenta*, vol. 4 *Sophocles* (Gottingen: Vandenhoeck & Ruprecht, 1977).

R. Rehm, *Marriage to Death: The Conflation of Wedding and Funeral Rituals in Greek Tragedy* (Princeton: Princeton University Press, 1994).

D.H. Roberts, 'Sophoclean Endings: Another Story', *Arethusa* 21 (1988), 177-96.

T.G. Rosenmeyer, *Senecan Drama and Stoic Cosmology* (Berkeley, Los Angeles and London: University of California Press, 1989).

R. Scodel, *Sophocles* (Boston: Twayne, 1984).

R. Seaford (ed.). *Euripides: Cyclops* (Oxford: Clarendon Press, 1984).

—— 'Wedding Ritual and Textual Criticism in Sophocles' "Women of Trachis" ', *Hermes* 114 (1986), pp. 50-9.

D. Seale, *Vision and Stagecraft in Sophocles* (Chicago: University of Chicago Press, 1982).

C. Segal, *Tragedy and Civilization: An Interpretation of Sophocles* (Cambridge, Massachusetts and London: Harvard University Press, 1981).

—— *Sophocles' Tragic World: Divinity, Nature, Society* (Cambridge and London: Harvard University Press, 1995).

C.E. Sorum, 'Monsters and the Family: the Exodos of Sophocles' *Trachiniae*', *Greek, Roman and Byzantine Studies* 19 (1978), 59-73.

T.C.W. Stinton, 'The Scope and Limits of Allusion in Greek Tragedy', pp. 67-102 in Cropp, M.J. et al. (eds), *Greek Tragedy and its Legacy: Essays Presented to D.J. Conacher* (Toronto: University of Toronto Press, 1986).

B.S. Strauss, *Fathers and Sons in Athens: Ideology and Society in the Era of the Peloponnesian War* (Princeton: Princeton University Press, 1993).

O. Taplin, *The Stagecraft of Aeschylus: The Dramatic Use of Exits and Entrances in Greek Tragedy* (Oxford: Oxford University Press, 1977).

——— *Greek Tragedy in Action* (London: Methuen, 1978).

J-P. Vernant and P. Vidal-Naquet, *Tragedy and Myth in Ancient Greece*, trans. Janet Lloyd. (Sussex and New Jersey: Harvester Press and Humanities Press, 1981; original French publication, 1972).

T.B.L. Webster, *An Introduction to Sophocles* (Oxford: Clarendon Press, 1936).

C.H. Whitman, *Sophocles: A Study of Heroic Humanism* (Cambridge, Massachusetts: Harvard University Press, 1966).

D. Wiles, *Tragedy in Athens: Performance Space and Theatrical Meaning* (Cambridge: Cambridge University Press, 1997).

——— *Greek Theatre Performance: An Introduction* (Cambridge: Cambridge University Press, 2000).

B. Williams, '*The Women of Trachis*: Fictions, Pessimism, Ethics', pp. 43-53 in R.B. Louden and P. Schollmeier (eds), *The Greeks and Us: Essays in Honour of Arthur W.H. Adkins* (Chicago, Illinois: University of Chicago Press, 1996).

C.K. Williams and G.W. Dickerson (trans.), *Sophocles: Women of Trachis* (New York and Oxford: Oxford University Press, 1978).

P. Wilson, *The Athenian Institution of the Khoregia: The Chorus, the City and the Stage* (Cambridge: Cambridge University Press, 2000).

J.J. Winkler and F. Zeitlin (eds), *Nothing to Do with Dionysos? Athenian Drama in its Social Context* (Princeton: Princeton University Press, 1990).

R.P. Winnington-Ingram, *Sophocles: An Interpretation* (Cambridge: Cambridge University Press, 1980).

V. Wohl, *Intimate Commerce: Exchange, Gender, and Subjectivity in Greek Tragedy* (Austin: University of Texas Press, 1998).

M. Xie, 'Pound as translator', pp. 214-17 in I.B. Nadel (ed.), *The Cambridge Companion to Ezra Pound* (Cambridge: Cambridge University Press, 1999).

# Glossary

*Anakaluptêria*. Part of a wedding ritual in which bride raised her veil and revealed her face to her husband.

**Apotheosis**. Deification; the elevation of a mortal to the status of a god.

*Daimôn*. Spirit, god.

*Damazein*. To tame.

*Damar*. Wife, concubine.

*Dêmos*. The people.

*Dikê*. Justice.

*Eisodos* (pl. *eisodoi*).Side entrance along which the Chorus and characters enter and exit.

*Ekdosis*. 'Giving away' of the bride, one of the key ceremonies in marriage.

*Ekhthros*. Personal enemy.

*Erôs*. Passionate erotic desire, often capitalised to personify as a god.

*Exodos*. Final episode of the drama.

*Kalumma* (pl. *kalummata*). A veil worn by brides, a covering.

*Khlaina*. A type of cloak.

*Khorêgos*. Wealthy Athenian who paid to train the Chorus.

*Kurios*. Master, head of family, legal guardian.

*Nostos* (pl. *nostoi*). A return; a typical story pattern in Greek literature.

*Oikos*. House, household, family.

*Orkhêstra*. Large, open area where the Chorus performed, between audience and skênê.

*Parodos*. First song of the Chorus, sung while entering the performance space.

*Philos* (pl. *philoi*). Friend, family member, associate.

*Phthonos*. Malice, envy.

*Polis* (pl. *poleis*). City-state, a politically autonomous city and surrounding land.

*Prologos*. The beginning of the drama (before the entrance of the Chorus).

*Skênê*. Wooden building at the back of the performance area into and out of which some entrances and exits are made; usually represents a house or palace.

*Sôphrosunê*. A virtue with a range of connotations, such as sexual restraint, deference, moderation, and self-control.

**Stasimon** (pl. **stasima**). 'Standing song', i.e. the choral songs after the Chorus has entered during the *parodos*.

**Timê**. Price, honour, status; the value of an individual in the eyes of the community.

# Chronology

**BC**
**508/7**: Political reforms of Cleisthenes.
*c.* **495**: Birth of Sophocles.
**484**: Aeschylus' first victory.
**480/79**: Greek city states defeat the Persians.
**468**: Sophocles' first production.
**458**: Production of Aeschylus' *Oresteia*.
*c.* **457 – *c*. 430**: *Women of Trachis* produced.
**456**: Death of Aeschylus.
**455**: Euripides' first production.
**431**: Outbreak of the Peloponnesian War between Athens and Sparta.
**406**: Death of Euripides.
**406/5**: Death of Sophocles
**404**: Sparta defeats Athens.
**end of 1st century**: Ovid's *Heroides* IX (poem).

**AD**
**after 65**: Senecan *Hercules Oetaeus* (drama).
**1464**: Raoul Le Fèvre's *Recueil des hystoires de Troyes* (medieval romance).
**1632**: Jean Rotrou's *Hercule mourant* (drama).
**1892**: Richard Jebb's commentary on the *Women of Trachis*.
**1953**: Ezra Pound's version of the *Women of Trachis*.
**1954**: Pound's version performed on the BBC.
**1959**: Pound's version performed in Darmstadt, Germany (director: Sellner).
**1960**: Pound's version performed in New York, USA.
**1967**: Archibald MacLeish's *Herakles* (drama).
**1976**: *Women of Trachis* staged in Köln, Germany (director: Heyme).

# Index

154

# Index